The 4ᵗʰ Musketeer

The 4th Musketeer

Living in the service of the King

Henk Stoorvogel
and Theo van den Heuvel

MONARCH
BOOKS

Oxford UK, and Grand Rapids, USA

English translation provided courtesy of Uitgeverij Kok, part of
VBK | Media B. V., Herculesplein 96. 3584 AA Utrecht, The
Netherlands.

Published by Monarch Books
an imprint of
Lion Hudson plc
Wilkinson House, Jordan Hill Road,
Oxford OX2 8DR, England
Email: monarch@lionhudson.com
www.lionhudson.com/monarch

ISBN 978 0 85721 674 8
e-ISBN 978 0 85721 675 5

First edition 2015

Acknowledgments
Unless otherwise stated Scripture quotations taken from the Holy
Bible, New International Version Anglicised. Copyright © 1979,
1984, 2011 Biblica, formerly International Bible Society. Used by
permission of Hodder & Stoughton Ltd, an Hachette UK company.
All rights reserved. "NIV" is a registered trademark of Biblica. UK
trademark number 1448790.
Scripture quotations marked NRSV are from The New Revised
Standard Version of the Bible copyright © 1989 by the Division
of Christian Education of the National Council of Churches in the
USA. Used by permission. All Rights Reserved.

A catalogue record for this book is available from the British Library

Printed and bound in the UK, July 2015, LH26

For Manuel, Chris, and Luca – our
three musketeers.
You are loved.
For who you are.

Contents

Foreword

If I were a young man again, I would have loved to to be a Musketeer.

I have a special affinity with the Muskathlon, since I once was an athlete myself, with a special talent for running. I even had an eye to the Olympics. But I was running in my own track, until during my army years in the Dutch Indies, now Indonesia, a bullet smashed up my ankle and I ended up in hospital. There nursing nuns showed such joy and love that I started asking them about it. They then spoke to me about the love of God and I finally started reading the Bible that my mother had given me when I left home two-and-a-half years before. Looking back at it all I am so happy that that bullet opened the door to the bigger "run" which at 87 is still going on! I was put in the track of Jesus and am running with and for Him.

Men, I encourage you to read this book and let the message sink in deep. Be sure to keep running in the track of Jesus. Be bold. Step out of your boat. Follow closely behind Jesus, who always walked in the will of His Father. Be inspired to become the man you were intended to be.

Brother Andrew
Founder and president emeritus of Open Doors, serving persecuted Christians worldwide
Harderwijk, The Netherlands, June 2015

Preface

The 4th Musketeer is a men's movement that organizes the Xtreme Character Challenges or XCC events. Twice a year, in the spring and autumn, a group of around 100 men – in teams of eight – embark on a journey into the wilderness. From Thursday evening to Sunday afternoon, these men are part of an adventure. The teams are given assignments that will test their ingenuity, courage, team spirit, stamina, and character. Each assignment is based on an idea. Thinking exercises are linked to the physical challenges, reflecting the principle that life lessons travel the longest distance possible... the distance from the mind to the heart.

In 2008, I (Henk) asked three of my best friends – Theo van den Heuvel, Jan Stoorvogel, and Pieter Cnossen – to spend an evening together. In the past, we had worked together with Athletes in Action in the Netherlands and had many unique experiences together. However, at that time, each of us lived in a different city and we didn't see each other very often. When you desire to maintain friendships, it is important to build a history together, continually enriching your shared past and increasing your prospects of a shared future. I asked my friends how they felt about establishing a men's movement: The 4th Musketeer. Our sports background taught us that physical challenges can also have a mental dimension, and together we designed the concept of the Xtreme Character Challenge.

In 2012, I (Henk) called my close friend in America, Kent Susud, who is the founder of SportQuest Ministries, and asked him to lead the charge... to bring this movement to America. Today, thousands of European and American men live in the spirit of the Musketeer. They have received their crimson red polo shirt imprinted with the white "four". We have seen God work in a personal and intense way. God has touched the hearts of men, and their lives will never be the same. The wives of Musketeers frequently tell us how much their husbands have changed because of these weekends. This fills our hearts with gratitude and gives us the energy to further expand The 4th Musketeer.

The 4th Musketeer not only inspires men, but we also call them to action. Through the Muskathlon, we currently have three strategic partnerships. We sponsor many fatherless children in Africa through Compassion International; we support the persecuted church in the Middle East with Open Doors; and we battle against human trafficking in Eastern Europe with A21. We believe that God doesn't entrust men with wealth and a nice family just to live in peace. Men have a responsibility that reaches beyond their small family. As stewards of the King, we may, can, and must give our lives for His purpose for our generation.

The Three Musketeers

The name of the men's movement The 4th Musketeer is inspired by the book *The Three Musketeers* written by Alexandre Dumas (1802). The story takes place in early seventeenth-century France. The 18-year-old nobleman d'Artagnan leaves his childhood home and moves to Paris, determined to become a musketeer. The musketeers were the elite troops of the French king, Louis XIII. The French king, married to Queen Anna, is a weak monarch, heavily influenced by Cardinal Richelieu, head of the Catholic

Church in France. Through trickery and deceit, Cardinal Richelieu tries to discredit the king to such an extent that he is able to depose him and rule over France. He is assisted in this by femme fatale Milady de Winter.

Athos, Aramis, and Porthos – the three musketeers – join forces with d'Artagnan to do everything in their power to prevent the cardinal from executing his plans and to protect the king. D'Artagnan is initially appointed guard, but is later promoted to musketeer as a reward for his heroic actions. He falls in love with the beautiful Constance, maid of honour to Queen Anna, but he also falls for the charms of the deceptive Milady.

The voluminous book – our Dutch version had 672 pages – is a delightful read. The four friends have the craziest adventures and engage in the most insane antics. In writing his book, Alexandre Dumas was himself inspired by the stories of musketeers from the sixteenth century.

The 4th Musketeer, the book

The famous phrase from the Dumas classic, "All for one and one for all", articulates how Jesus has dealt with us and how we wish to deal with each other. In fact, *The Three Musketeers* mainly revolves around the fourth musketeer, d'Artagnan. He is the protagonist, the true hero of the story. We join him on his journey from his childhood home into the world, from boy to man, from guard to musketeer.

In a sense, we are all the fourth musketeer. Each of us is on a journey through life, from boy to man.

The idea for this book was born from a desire to shape and substantiate exactly that: it is all for one and one for all, and *you* are the true hero in the journey from boy to man, in the story of your life, at the service of the King.

Each chapter begins with a brief quote from *The Three Musketeers.* The quote will not be explained, but it is most definitely connected to the contents of the chapter. To discover the connection, reading *The 4th Musketeer* is not enough; you'll have to read *The Three Musketeers* as well.

Should you want more information on The 4th Musketeer or to join one of our Xtreme Character Challenges or the Muskathlon, please visit our website at www.the4thmusketeer.org.

We wish you many blessings in reading this book.

For the King!

Henk and Theo

Prologue

The boy with the hessian sack

A little boy and his old father set out to climb a tall mountain. They were accompanied by a bull and a raven. The small group struggled to find their way up the steep slope. A few trees offered them some shelter and something to grip, but otherwise this was a place for gods, not for men. The boy was carrying a heavy hessian sack. His father was a potato farmer and — if nothing else — they had to be able to eat on top of the mountain. So his father told him to bring the hessian sack, packed with potatoes.

The boy insisted on taking the bull with them on their adventure. The father thought it was strange. Who climbs a mountain with a bull? But the son was adamant. So the bull tagged along, although the bull itself didn't understand it either.

The raven joined of its own initiative. He was often found sitting on the fence that separated the potato field from the small farm where the father and his son lived. When the raven saw that the old man and his son were about to travel, he jumped up from his fence and flew with them.

The climb was heavy and slow. The path had given way first to gravel and then to hard, smooth rock miles ago. The higher they climbed, the steeper the mountain was. Before long, there wouldn't be any trees around them, and beyond that, there would be perpetual snow and treacherous ice.

"I need to rest for a while," the old man gasped, and he squatted down against the last tree before the endless void of the mountain summit. The bull seemed happy and tried to stand still on a large slippery rock. The raven perched on a low-hanging branch. The boy placed his heavy sack on the ground and started massaging his painful shoulder, as he felt the sweat dripping from his forehead.

"There's a storm coming," the old man said as he pointed his crooked finger upwards. "We need to head back."

"But father," the boy answered, "I don't want to go back. I want to climb this mountain."

"If we go on, this mountain will be the death of us," the father said, and he closed his eyes. "We're going back."

"Please, have a potato, Father. You'll feel much better."

The old man didn't answer. He simply shook his head gently. There was silence for a moment. Then the father opened his eyes, looked at his boy, and said, "Son, we're heading back. This mountain is too dangerous, too steep, too high. You are too small to climb this mountain, and I am too old. And a storm is coming."

The boy bit his lip. A tear formed in his eyes, crawled over the edge of his eyelid, and slowly rolled down. "Father, I'm going to keep on climbing. I want to climb this mountain. It has been my dream from the very moment I saw it for the first time."

The boy lifted the sack back onto his shoulder, walked towards the bull, grabbed his rope, and wrapped it around his right wrist, twice. Then he started climbing alone, leaving his father behind. The raven jumped up from his branch and flew with the boy, with the bull following closely behind. He started to feel a cold wind blowing, with no shrubs or shelter anywhere around to protect him. Clouds gathered at the top, resembling the line of defence of a besieged city, ready to throw any attacker into the abyss. Nobody saw the tears of the boy. Nobody saw the tears of the old man.

As he kept on climbing, the boy noticed that his sack was starting to feel lighter. How was that possible? He decided that the bull had probably stolen a meal. He continued on bravely towards the clouds that kept growing wilder and darker.

The storm swallowed him up, devoured him as if he were a potato in the mouth of the bull. He dropped to his knees to prevent himself from being blown off the mountain, and then he started crawling, holding on to pinnacles and ledges. The howling of the storm drowned out the howling of his scared bull. The bull started to slip more and more. Their situation was becoming increasingly precarious. If the boy wanted to save his bull, there was only one solution: They had to climb back down.

The boy kept climbing determinedly upwards. This time, the mountain was his. The inevitable happened in a blink. The bull slipped again, but this time, he failed to find his footing. The rope cut into the hand of the boy, and he almost lost his sack of potatoes. Because the rope was wrapped round his wrist, he was unable to let go even if he wanted to. The falling bull started to drag the boy with him into the abyss. The boy struggled with all his strength, braced himself, and screamed with effort. The tightly stretched rope scraped across a sharp ledge, parted, and suddenly the boy fell back against the mountainside. The sudden impact made the sack hit the rock, and along with the bull several pounds of precious potatoes fell into the fathomless depth.

Dazed, the boy lay on the ground as the storm attempted to blow him into the abyss as well. As he lay there, he lost track of time, but eventually he carefully got back onto his hands and knees. He swung the hessian sack with the remaining potatoes across his shoulder and started crawling again. Was it his imagination, or did the storm seem less violent than before? He kept crawling on autopilot: right hand, left knee; left hand, right knee. Inch by inch, he approached the top.

Suddenly, all was silent. The clouds had disappeared. The wind had dropped. The small boy with the sack looked up, and about 30 feet above him, he saw the last bit of mountain giving way to endless sky. He got to his feet and walked the last few yards to the top. Minutes later, he had reached the place he had always dreamed of: the rooftop of his world. Everywhere around him, he saw the snow-covered majestic mountaintops. There he was, alone, between heaven and earth. Alone? The boy looked again. Above him, below him, next to him... the raven was nowhere to be found. Probably blown away by the lashing storm, just like the bull. And so many of his costly potatoes. Potatoes! Suddenly, the boy realized that he felt like eating a potato. He had most certainly earned one. He pulled the strangely lightweight sack from his shoulder and looked into it. Empty! During his final climb, the sack had got caught on a sharp rock and been torn open. All of the potatoes were gone. Food for the ravens and the bulls. The boy looked up with the purest smile possible. Who cares about potatoes when you're at the top of a mountain?

The boy sat down, allowing himself to enjoy the magnificent view to the fullest. He drank in the splendour of creation like the sweetest nectar. Gradually, the setting sun turned the blue sky, snow-covered mountaintops, and green forests to a pink and golden angelic jubilation, formed to sing about the greatness of God. And as the boy was sitting there, he saw it appear, right before the setting sun, graciously gliding in the glorious ocean of light: the eagle.

The boy got up and stretched his stiffened muscles. It was time to go home. He carefully climbed down, leaving the torn hessian sack at the top.

(For a commentary on this parable, see p. 42)

I

OUR STORY

This book is not a random sequence of unrelated chapters. It is a whole, and it tells a story. It is the story of the boy with the hessian sack, en route to becoming a man with a mission.

Similarly, our lives are not a random sequence of unrelated encounters and situations. Each of our lives is a cohesive book. Every chapter builds on the last one and affects the next one. Our lives tell a story. We *are* a story. More often than we realize, where we come from affects our future and shapes what drives us.

What is your story? For whom do you live?

The answers to these questions are vital. They make us receptive to the healing voice from heaven. They expose our deepest motives and biggest dreams, which are often less related to God than we'd like to admit. And they open our lives to beauty and friendship in a surprising way.

1

Why Alexander Supertramp died

I speak of Monsieur de Tréville, who was formerly my neighbor, and who had the honor to be, as a child, the play-fellow of our king, Louis XIII, whom God preserve!... in spite of edicts, ordinances, and decrees, there he is, captain of the Musketeers; that is to say, chief of a legion of Caesars, whom the king holds in great esteem and whom the cardinal dreads – he who dreads nothing, as it is said. Still further, Monsieur de Tréville gains ten thousand crowns a year; he is therefore a great noble. He began as you begin. Go to him with this letter, and make him your model in order that you may do as he has done.

ALEXANDRE DUMAS

In the spring of 1990, Chris McCandless disappeared from the lives of his parents. The 22-year-old recent college graduate refused to settle for a life of career hunting and materialism. "Working on a career," Chris condescendingly told his parents, "is nothing but an inferior invention of the twentieth century. It's more of a burden than an advantage."

He gave all of his savings – about $20,000 – to a charity, to benefit the poor. He climbed into his old yellow Datsun and off he went, chasing his dreams. To symbolize his new lifestyle, he assumed a new name: Alexander Supertramp. After he lost his car, due to a sudden flood in a riverbed in the desert, he hitchhiked across the US to the Southwest. Using a canoe, he paddled to Mexico. Later, he worked in the endless grain fields of South Dakota. He survived in the most remote areas with minimal food and water. Chris had a dream. He wanted to live – with a capital L. And he was sure about one thing: his parents didn't understand what living was all about.

His father, Walt, played a major role in Chris's decision to turn his life around radically. It's not that Walt was a bad or violent father. Walt was a brilliant NASA scientist. Chris's mother was the love of Walt's life, but she was his second wife. Although Walt invested a lot into his relationship with Chris ("I never played and did as much with the other children"), Chris became disillusioned. During a previous trip, in his student days, he discovered that his father had not divorced his first wife until well after he had already been living comfortably with Chris's mother. Walt had secretly led two lives for quite some time. That was years ago, but Chris couldn't forgive his father for his betrayal. He compared all of his father's statements and actions to the period of infidelity he had discovered. Chris didn't want to be like his father, so he started searching. Initiated a quest in search of meaning... of himself. Or, was he simply running?

Quest

To Franz, an old man Chris met during his journeys, he wrote:

*The most basic of human mental strength is the
desire for adventure. Our joy of living is the result
of our encounters with what's new, meaning
that there is no greater pleasure than constantly
seeing a changing horizon, and walking under a
new and different sun every single day.*

Chris's struggle with his father led him to seek out the ruggedness of Alaska. He wanted to survive by himself in unspoiled nature. In April 1992, Chris followed his heart, hitchhiked, and journeyed into the Alaskan wilderness. In Denali National Park, he found an old green city bus... an International Harvester from the 1940s. A mining company left the bus there when they discovered that it wasn't possible to build a road into the heart of the wilderness, and it was now serving as a shelter for hunters and adventurers. Chris took up residence in the bus and hunted ducks, squirrels, and porcupines. He even managed to shoot a moose!

As the weather improved, food became scarcer, and Chris decided to return to the inhabited world. However, his path was cut off by the fast-flowing Teklanika River, fed by melting mountain ice water. The adventurer was forced to return to the bus, and he became weaker and weaker.

On 6 September 1994, six people happened to hike past the antique green bus. The hunters and hikers found a letter, stating:

*S.O.S. I need your help. I am hurt, nearly dead,
and too weak to leave this place. I am all by
myself. This isn't a joke. Please stay here and save*

*me. I am nearby, trying to find berries, and I will
be back tonight. Thank you, Chris McCandless.
August?*

Strikingly, the letter was signed *Chris McCandless*.
Apparently, he had decided to reassume his true name. In
addition, it was clear that the letter had been written at
least a week earlier, on some day in August. Where had
Chris gone?

David, the hobbit

Deep inside, Chris's adventurous journey was related to his
complex relationship with his father. Several well-known
biblical characters also had to struggle with a crisis with
their fathers at a young age. Moses, for instance, was forced
to grow up without his biological father. Joseph was spoiled
so much by his father that his brothers began hating him.
And of course, there is David – the man after God's heart.
In 1 Samuel 16:1–13, we encounter him for the first time.
Samuel is travelling to the little town of Bethlehem to anoint
a new king. Nowadays, everyone knows Bethlehem as the
place where Jesus was born, adjacent to the spiritual capital
of the world, Jerusalem. But, in Samuel's time, Bethlehem
was an insignificant mountain village, somewhat like Lost
Springs, Wyoming. The great Samuel travels from the big
city to Bethlehem to anoint a new king. In today's world, it
would be the equivalent of U2 lead singer Bono landing in
Lost Springs. The entire village is in turmoil.

Is this positive or negative? A little bit of both. From the
negative viewpoint, Israel is facing a crisis. In a moral sense,
the people are being increasingly eroded. Everyone simply
does whatever they want. There is no unity, no holiness.

There is no perspective. There is a king – Saul – but his personality is unfit for his crown. And that's just the internal side of the story. Externally, there are some significant challenges as well... primarily with the Philistines. The Philistines are the elephants and the Israelites are the mice. The Philistines have a monopoly on iron, live in cities, and race around in tank-like chariots. The Israelites have hardly any iron weapons, live mostly in tents, and run across the battlefield with wooden pitchforks. And the worst thing is: The Philistines produce giants.

In the midst of this crisis, Samuel must anoint a new king. God has told Samuel that He has chosen a son of Jesse to become the new king. He arrives in Bethlehem and invites the village elders, along with Jesse and all of his sons, for a feast. During this meal, we witness the infliction of a painful father wound. As each of Jesse's sons is introduced to Samuel, the answer of God is consistently clear: "This is not him." All seven sons that came to the dinner with Jesse have been reviewed, and the chosen one is not among them. Samuel didn't get it. Had he misunderstood God? Are there more people named Jesse in Bethlehem? Confused, he asks Jesse whether these are all of his sons. The old man turns red and somewhat nervously plucks at his beard. "Eh, well, I don't know how to say this. I have another son, the *haqqaton*. He is outside with the sheep."

Excuse me? Jesse had eight sons. Not seven, but eight! And on the most important day of the year in the sleepy town of Bethlehem... the day that every young man has dreamed of: the day of the *choice*, possibilities, *life*... Jesse simply does not invite one of his sons. The history of Bethlehem can be subdivided into the period prior to the visit of Samuel and the period thereafter, and at that supreme moment, Jesse doesn't even bother calling in his son.

Amid all of his brothers, Samuel, and the village elders, Jesse presents his son as the *haqqaton*. It is not a nice word. It means the "little one", the "runt", the "*hobbit*". They are the first words a person uses to describe David in the Bible: "the *hobbit*". A name used by his father. The *hobbit* for a 16-year-old boy, in a society where you reach manhood at the age of 12. The *hobbit* for a boy who had conquered both a lion and a bear.

Some scholars believe that David wasn't summoned because he was far away, in the fields with the sheep, and that it was impossible to call him. However, David wasn't far away at all. Samuel says: "All well and good, but we won't start eating before David has arrived." Within seconds, David is brought in, together with a trace of sheep smell. That is the beginning of David's story: belittled, humiliated, skipped during the supreme moment, by his very own father.

That scars a man.

Cinderella

There may be more to this story, though. There is a chance that David may have been the product of an affair of his father. Twice, the Bible explicitly states that David has "reddish" hair. Apparently, he didn't look like his brothers. We repeatedly read that David's brothers hate their (step) brother, even though David is good and brave. The name of David's mother is never mentioned once, whereas it is mentioned for the other kings of Judah. The army commanders of David are not – as you would expect – his brothers, but Abishai, Joab, and Asahel, his nephews. Isaiah speaks prophetically about the birth of Jesus as if he is talking about a shoot that will come out of the severed trunk of Jesse, a "sprout from his roots". A "sprout" is a wild offshoot that shoots from the root next to the trunk. It has the same roots, but it is still of different origin.

On the other hand, the name *David* means "beloved", "dear". So somewhere deep inside, David must also be wanted by his father and/or mother.

Be that as it may, in the first scene we read about him, David is presented as the Cinderella of Jesse's family. A (step)son with seven older brothers who clearly don't like him and a father who doesn't defend him at all. On the contrary, Jesse consistently seems to present David as *the hobbit.* Good for nothing but sheepherding.

Speaking is living; silence is death

How does one deal with so much hostility? How do you process a trauma in such a way that it makes you stronger in the end? How do you prevent yourself from being paralysed, ultimately missing all of your life's goals?

Dan P. McAdams, a renowned psychologist, claims that two things are important to help you to process your trauma in a way that makes your personal story stronger. The first is your ability to *honestly face and name your wound*. The second is your ability to *share the wound with others*, through prayer, conversation, or in other ways. McAdams's findings are no different than what David did. In Psalm 27:10, David prays: "Even though my father and mother have left me, the Lord still accepts me."

It contains both elements. How did David feel about the way that he was treated by his father and mother? He felt abandoned, alone, betrayed. He faces his pain, and he shapes it into a prayer, so that he doesn't have to keep it to himself, but is able to share it with God. In Psalm 69, he expresses his inner pain about his relationship with his brothers: "I have become a stranger to my brothers, an unknown person to the sons of my mother."

Facing, naming, and sharing: That is the road to life. Remember the note from Chris that was found by the hunters on 6 September, attached to the green van in the Alaskan wilderness? They had noticed a smell in the vicinity of the bus. When they looked inside the bus, they found Chris in his sleeping bag – dead.

The people who got to know Chris McCandless during his two-year quest all tell the same story: Chris didn't want to say anything about his family or his deepest motives. Chris had decided to resolve his pain by himself. This decision tragically led to his death. The road to life involves true communication. If you decide to keep your pain and your problems to yourself, you will die – either literally or figuratively.

David's honesty and open communication about his past allowed God to work in his life in such a way that his potential weakness turned into his strength. When David, years after being anointed, is on the run from King Saul, he seeks shelter in a cave in the desert of Adullam. Before long, hundreds of other refugees arrive to keep him company, among them his parents and brothers. They have now turned to him for help and protection. The attackers have now become the persecuted; the tyrants have become the refugees. *It's payback time.* How will David respond?

David takes his parents to safety with a king he has befriended and takes his brothers under his wing.

He cares. He forgives.

My story

Maybe it's about time I (Henk) told you a little more about the role of my father in my life.

When my mother was pregnant with me, my biological father ran off.

Various factors played a role in this, but the fact was that I was born into a single parent family and I never had any contact with my biological father. When I was two, my mother married the man who I call my father. My mother and my new father had four more children, and we were one big happy family. However, in the background, the fact that my biological father had left us kept eating at me. In my teens, there were periods when I was extremely angry with him. He had run off and abandoned my mother and me. It was a wondrous mix of feelings. On one hand, I had the homey happiness of a family with a sweet father and mother, and on the other hand, I had the hole created by the departure of my biological father.

When I was married, and Ruth – my wife – was expecting our firstborn, the desire to meet my biological father increased. After months of investigation, we finally found his address. Koen (not his real name) had meanwhile retired and was living in Limburg. I wrote him a letter, asking him if he would be willing to meet me. It would be the first contact we ever had. Koen wrote back to me with a positive response. I called him. Heard his voice. We agreed to meet at a restaurant in Amersfoort. I was there first. Nervous. Koen arrived shortly after, and we clumsily embraced each other.

There were two things I wanted from this meeting. First, I wanted to forgive Koen for the fact that he had abandoned me. Maybe he felt remorse, and I wanted him to be able to spend his last years on earth in peace. Secondly, I wanted to know who he was and to find out whether there was any foundation for building a relationship.

The conversation was one big deception.

Koen didn't want or need my forgiveness. He was fine with the idea of us being in touch after all these years. He wanted me to tell him what I wanted. There was nothing in his behaviour that told me that he was eager, that he wanted *me.* Somewhere inside, I had hoped that he wanted to get to know me and that he was willing to run the risk of crossing my boundaries. But Koen didn't take any risks.

It was my first and only encounter with Koen.

Our inner rift directs our lives

In *Wild at Heart*, Christian author and speaker John Eldredge speaks about the "father wound". The German Benedictine Father Anselm Grun describes the same phenomenon as "inner conflict". Many men, including us, recognize that rift in our own lives. Whether your pain is in your relationship with your father, your mother, or an older brother, most of us face a deep, inner pain with a close family member.

A man told me (Henk): "My father always had other things that were more important than me, or at least that's how he made me feel. Once, I was rocking in my chair and fell backwards. The first thing that my father checked was whether or not the floor was dented. After that, he asked me how I was doing."

Another man told me (Henk): "My father was always working. Six days a week, in the morning, the afternoon, the evening. He either worked or he played soccer. Sunday afternoon was his only afternoon off. He would be sleeping on the sofa. He loved soccer. But I can't remember him ever watching one of my games."

We could add countless stories to this collection: stories of harsh fathers who were much too abusive with their hands, or feet; stories of harsh, extremely religious fathers who were only focused on God's holiness and justice; stories of drinking, non-communicative, or absent fathers; and stories of sick, dominant, wasteful, or manipulative mothers.

What is your story?

That is an important question. What is your story? Because we all live in a story. We *are* a story. We carry our story with us, like a snail carries around its house. Our life in the present is a response to our past, and it is our initial offer towards the future. Psychologists have long thought that man is a set of properties or a combination of behaviours. Nowadays, more and more psychologists have reached the conclusion that man, above all, is *a story* and lives in his own story. Based on that story, properties and behaviours are created. Ultimately, our story is formed in response to a number of people in our immediate vicinity, who play a decisive role in our life. For most people, these are fathers, mothers, brothers, or sisters. Our story is a result of the desire to be accepted, loved, seen by them, or an attempt to find a place to conceal pain and wounds from the past. Our deepest motives and biggest dreams are often less related to God than we would be willing to admit.

2

Preaching for my father

Never fear quarrels, but seek adventures. I
have taught you how to handle a sword; you
have thews of iron, a wrist of steel. Fight on
all occasions. Fight the more for duels being
forbidden, since consequently there is twice
as much courage in fighting. I have nothing to
give you, my son, but fifteen crowns, my horse,
and the counsels you have just heard... Take
advantage of all, and live happily and long.

ALEXANDRE DUMAS

If there's any country in the world that knows how to make
a great sports movie, it's the United States. Which is why I
(Henk) asked some American friends a couple of years ago
what the best sports movie was that they had ever seen.
The unanimous answer was *Rudy*. The movie tells the true
story of Daniel "Rudy" Ruettiger, the son of a factory worker
from Joliet, a small town in Illinois. A simple shepherd from
Bethlehem.

The father and brothers of Rudy are crazy about the
Notre Dame football team... the only team they are allowed

to watch on television in the Ruettiger residence. It creates a dream in Rudy's heart: he wants to play football for the University of Notre Dame, a very expensive institution with one of the best football teams in the country. It is a great dream. However, reality is not in Rudy's favour: he is far too small to be a football player (only 5 foot 6 inches), has little talent, lacks the grades to qualify for a scholarship, and has no money. His father and brothers keep trying to talk him out of his dream and to convince him that he wasn't born to be a football player, but simply to live his life in the local steel factory, just like them. However, Rudy refuses to give up on his dream. He ends his relationship with his girlfriend and travels to Notre Dame. He expresses his motives as follows:

Ever since I was a little boy, I dreamed about going to school here, and all that time, everybody told me that it was impossible. All my life, people have been telling me what and what not to do. I have always listened to them and believed what they said. But I don't want that any more.

By starting his college education at a smaller university, Rudy manages to get grades that are just good enough to be accepted into the university of his dreams. He has no money to pay for a room so he sleeps in the equipment room of the football team. Although his chances of making the team are slim, he succeeds in doing so... not because of his size or talent, but because of his perseverance. He doesn't care about scratches, bumps, bruises, or bleeding. His training intensity becomes proverbial, and, as a sparring partner for the core team, he becomes an important factor in the team's success. However, he is never selected, because he is too small for the real deal.

In preparation for his last year, he gathers all of his courage and asks his coach whether he can play one game in his team uniform, sitting on the bench. His reason?

> *My father loves Notre Dame football more than anything. He doesn't believe that I'm on the team, because he can't see me on the bench during the matches. Next year, my last year, I would like to give this to him as a gift: I would really appreciate it if you would allow me to get onto the field just once with the team.*

Coach Ara asks whether this is his only reason. Rudy replies:

> *No. No, it is for everyone who told me that it was impossible to play football for Notre Dame. It is for my brothers and the boys at my high school and the guys I worked with in the steel mill. They can't attend the training and see that I'm part of the team.*

The coach promises to select him, but he leaves the team shortly thereafter and the new coach refuses to keep the promise of his predecessor. The team captains speak up for Rudy, and in their last home game, he is given the honour of leading the team onto the field. When his father enters the stadium of Notre Dame for the first time in his life to watch his son play, he gets emotional and says: "This is the most beautiful thing these eyes have ever seen." Rudy is with the team. However, he is not given any playing time. The players start chanting Rudy's name and the audience copies them. Thousands of voices chant: "Rudy, Rudy, Rudy." The coach has no other option than to acquiesce, and in the very last minute of the game, Rudy is allowed onto the field. He is allowed to run two *plays*, and in the last play, he manages to tackle the quarterback of the opposing team with the ball. Rudy's team members carry him on their shoulders: an homage that no player of Notre Dame has ever seen since Rudy. The urge to show your father or brothers what you are capable of can lead a man to go to great lengths.

Is the world ruled by orphans?

What the stories of d'Artagnan, Chris, and Rudy all have in common is that their relationships with their fathers drove these young men to make radical choices and huge sacrifices. They are not alone. Psychologist Marvin Eisenstadt, along with several of his colleagues, conducted a massive study into the reason why some people become brilliant. From the most prominent encyclopedias in the world, they selected the 1,000 people who were given the most attention. These 1,000 greatest minds ever produced by mankind were examined for similarities. The outcome was both unexpected and striking. The ultimate factor revealed by the study? These great minds from the history of mankind had become orphans significantly younger than people with normal performances. The results were so compelling that the researchers even suggested this question: *Is our world ruled by orphans?*

People such as Dante Alighieri, Jean Jacques Rousseau, Edgar Allen Poe, Dostoyevsky, Tolstoy, Voltaire, Wordsworth, and many others have in common that they lost one or both parents during their childhood or teens. And it didn't stop there. A majority of Nobel Prize winners, 60 per cent of British prime ministers, Napoleon, and ten of the twelve Roman emperors suffered an early loss of their father and/ or mother.

Why do orphans excel? One of the reasons given by psychologists is the idea that some people use their loss or pain to overcompensate, to show the world – and maybe themselves first – that their life does, in fact, matter; that they are wanted, desired, and important. And they have a point! However, it is also important to realize that there are other people who suffer similar traumas, but they fail to convert this into positive energy and instead turn bitter and become emotionally paralysed.

One of the 1,000 "greatest minds on earth" studied was Alexandre Dumas, author of *The Three Musketeers*. When he was four years old, he lost his father. According to some, his masterpiece about the heroics of the musketeers is a reflection of his own ambitions and dreams. The story of d'Artagnan is thought to be his own story. And d'Artagnan is no exception; his father plays a large role in his life. The big drive behind the motives of d'Artagnan was… exactly, his father. His father had lived next door to Lord de Tréville before he became captain of the musketeers. And now, d'Artagnan's father had sent his son to Captain de Tréville to become what he was never able to become himself. In his son, d'Artagnan's father sees the opportunity to finally bring some glory to his own failed life. D'Artagnan embarks on his quest. He wants to become a musketeer. For whom? For King Louis XIII, of course. But just for him? Of course not.

Life as the eldest son

Many men know what it feels like to have dreams. Often, these dreams are related to their father or mother, even though some men don't realize it. Sometimes, men have had to face a weak father, and they promise themselves:

"I will not quit as easily as my father did." They have become strong men who never give up. They can be rough on themselves, and they often achieve great goals by doing so. Unfortunately, it also often means that they are too harsh on their immediate surroundings as well. Like Chris, who left his family behind without any further communication. Or Rudy, who gave up his girlfriend in order to follow his dream.

On the other hand, many men also know what it means to give up on their dreams, under pressure from fathers, mothers, or brothers. "That's just not for people like us. Act normally; that's crazy enough." Rudy's older brother had more talent than Rudy. However, he listened to his father and chose a life as a factory worker in the steel mill. Giving up his dream didn't mean that he didn't exist any more, but he was also hardly "alive". His cynical comments to Rudy tell the truth behind his own story. He has listened to his father and stayed home, but the warmth has left his life.

Many men live the story of the elder son instead of the prodigal younger son. The younger son spread his wings and chased his dreams. The elder son stayed behind and tried to live up to his ideas of what his father expected of him. Every day that the elder son survived the routine lifestyle of his father's estate made him more bitter. He was home, but without his heart. He lived a life of anger, resentment, and bitterness. And, in the end, the elder son was truly farther away from home than the younger.

Some of us climb mountains and reach high peaks. Others quit halfway and return. And somewhere along the road, for many of us, all of those choices are related to our father, mother, or brothers.

For whom are you preaching?

My (Henk's) dream is to become an international speaker and author – to communicate, to inspire, to share life as broadly and as deeply as possible. Just as Rudy wanted to show his father, brothers, and classmates all the things that he could do, I also have various intersecting motives. A while ago, I was talking to a communications expert. We were at a pleasant restaurant overlooking Het Loo Palace, enjoying a nice lunch while talking about the influence of preaching and the thesis study I was conducting about the transformative power of preaching. In the middle of the conversation, the communications expert suddenly looked me straight in the eye and asked: "And who is it you're preaching for? And for whom are you conducting this thesis study?"

I started out just fine. Christian. "Well, first of all, I'm doing it for God. Or at least, that is my deepest desire. And speaking happens to be one of the few things I'm good at, so I would like to perfect those skills." The 63-year-old communications expert kept looking at me, with a twinkle in his silver-grey eyes, waiting for me to give him a more honest answer.

"But if I truly take a deep look inside," I continued, "I would like my father to be proud of me. A hundred people can pay me a compliment after a sermon, but the one I truly need to hear it from is my father."

There was a silence.

The silver-grey eyes looked at me.

And then he said: "So, you only preach for your father, isn't that true? When I'm in the audience, you don't preach for me. You only preach for your father, even when he's not there."

"Well, I don't know. I also want to preach for God," I protested.

"You don't like me saying this. I can tell," the communications expert insisted.

"How can you tell?" I asked him.

"You just rubbed your eye with your finger, which means that you really don't want to hear what I'm saying."

"It's true. I don't like hearing it," I admitted, "but I do appreciate it. It allows me to do something about it."

It *is* true. I *would* like for my father (not my biological father that I told you about in the previous chapter, but the man I have been able to call my father since I was two) to be proud of me. Period. It is good to be aware of that. I don't live for God alone. I also live for a couple of people whose opinion is incredibly important to me.

I (Theo) recognize the same in my own life. I sent my first sermons to my father, who is a pastor, for correction. I was afraid to climb on stage without his approval. It sounds very pious to claim that you live for God alone, but it is much wiser to admit that the truth about your life is more nuanced. If you tell yourself that God alone is the source of all your motives, then you cease all discussions about your choices. After all, you do what you do because God asks you to. If your partner questions your choices, this would mean that she is going against God Himself. When you believe that God is the only one who directs you, there is a good chance that you're (subconsciously) making people around you suffer. Once you realize that you are actually being driven by a mixture of motives, you will give yourself (and the people around you) the opportunity to get closer to God's destination for your life. Your wife and good friends can then question your deepest motives, and you can then admit that you took that job and accept those endless working weeks to prove yourself to your father. And why sacrifice the happiness of your wife or your children to your need to be accepted by your father?

Leaving father and mother

First and last words are always given an extra emphasis. The first chapters of the Bible are much more than a simple description about the start of life on earth. They indicate how everything works at the core. The creation by God tells us that all life has intrinsic value, with people at the top of the hierarchy. The fall of man provides us with insight into the "why" of the fundamental brokenness in the world. And, in addition, those first three chapters describe essential aspects of the nature of man. In the context of the male–female relationship, the Bible says: "That is why a man leaves his father and mother and is united to his wife, and they become one flesh" (Genesis 2:24).

It is a well-known, but still remarkable, text. Why doesn't it say: "That is why a man and woman will leave their fathers and mothers, unite and become one flesh"?

Why is it the man who has to leave his father and mother? Isn't this something that should have also been said to the woman? Look at the proverbial *mother-in-law* of any random man. Mothers and daughters – now that is a relationship that the Bible should say something about. Still, in Genesis, the man is addressed specifically. Apparently, God thought that this was necessary. Where it sometimes seems as if the relationship between a man and his parents doesn't greatly affect his life and isn't something that requires special attention, the Bible starts issuing advice with regard to this exact relationship. Men! Leave your father and mother! And give yourself completely to your wife. From the moment that you two unite, she is more important than what your father and mother think about you. The call to the man to leave his father and mother doesn't necessarily mean an increase in geographical distance. That is the least important aspect of leaving his parents. It is about letting go of the (often unsaid) subconscious expectations and direction-setting role that parents play in the life of their son.

Did your father think that you were a slacker? And are you now building the most successful companies to prove him wrong, thereby having to work so much that your wife suffers from it?

Leave your father and mother.

Was your father a weak man, and did you promise yourself to become a strong man? If so, have you become so bold that you not only overstep your own boundaries, but also those of your wife and children?

Leave your father and mother.

Was your father a worrier? Did he always tell you not to make any irresponsible choices and never to take great risks? Has this led to you remaining afraid to chase after that dream that still resides in the catacombs of your heart?

Leave your father and mother.

Releasing yourself

You can't release yourself from your father and mother until you come to the realization that you're still attached to them. The Bible calls upon us men to choose a new family structure over the old family forms. Your wife switches places with your parents. For many men, that leap is so big that they are afraid to make it. Although they are married and have children, they subconsciously keep fighting for the appreciation of their father. Countless men have sacrificed their wife and children to satisfy their desire to meet the expectations of their father or mother at last. "All entrepreneurs are, in fact, insecure men," entrepreneurs have told me several times. What is the main reason that they build big companies, drive expensive cars, and are never satisfied with what they have? Often they say: "My father." As a man told me (Henk):

> *Finally I was able to buy a nice car. I was so proud.*
> *Now, my father could finally see that I had "made*
> *it". I showed the car to my father, and all he said*
> *was: "And now make sure you get to keep it."*

In some men, the dominance of their father or mother is evident. You can easily see why these men have become either a copy or an opposite of their father. It's also possible that your parents have treated you well and allowed you to do what you want, but that you, as their son, still involve them in your inner considerations. By honestly talking to your parents about your drives and motives, you might learn that there is more space deep inside than you're giving yourself (and your family).

The boy with the hessian sack could have listened to his father, like the elder son. If he had done that, he wouldn't have reached the peak of his mountain. The bull – a symbol of the anger and aggression in the boy – would have remained inside him. The raven – a symbol of death and loneliness – would not have left him. The boy was facing a crucial decision: "Will I stay a boy, or will I choose to become a man, even if my path to manhood means that I have to face a raging storm?" The boy chose the most difficult path... and found his life.

3

Thou shalt hate

"But you are not one of us," said Porthos.
"That's true," replied d'Artagnan; "I have not the
uniform, but I have the spirit. My heart is that of a
Musketeer; I feel it, monsieur, and that impels me on."

ALEXANDRE DUMAS

Like us, Jesus had an earthly father. Jesus' life was so strongly affected by Joseph the carpenter that He followed in the footsteps of His earthly father, as was customary back then. However, Jesus showed us what it means to leave your father and mother and to shape a new primary relationship in your life. When you study the texts about Jesus and His parents, you'll learn that His relationship with them was ambivalent, to say the least. That started at a very early age. When He joins his parents on a trip to Jerusalem as a 12-year-old boy, He deliberately stays behind at the table in the temple. It takes His parents three days of searching to find Him. The 12-year-old Jesus didn't feel the need to find His parents or to inform them of the fact that He wanted to remain in the temple a little longer. He simply stayed. When His parents, worried to death, finally find Him, they respond as any parent would after finding their lost child on a crowded beach:

> *His mother said to him, "Son, why have you*
> *treated us like this? Your father and I have been*
> *anxiously searching for you." (Luke 2:48)*

It is the response of a mother who is worried sick. However, Jesus seems unaffected by His mother's worries and responds reproachfully:

> *"Why were you searching for me?"... "Didn't you*
> *know I had to be in my Father's house?" (Luke*
> *2:49)*

It almost sounds rude. And it is understandable that Joseph and Mary didn't comprehend Jesus' response. "His Father's house? There was no carpenter's workshop in there! What was he talking about?"

This is the only story that we have about Jesus in his teens. There's a good reason why that one scene is about creating space in the relationships between a young man and his father and mother. In the rest of the Gospels, Joseph no longer plays a direct role. Maybe he died while Jesus was still young. Moreover, the fact that a parent has passed away does not prevent men from shaping their lives based on the (assumed) wishes of the deceased.

The next episode in which Jesus is presented with a parent, his mother, is just as painful as the situation in the temple. Jesus is attending a wedding in Cana with a couple of followers, when suddenly they appear to be out of wine. Mary, who is convinced that her son Jesus can help (even though He had never performed a miracle), walks over to Jesus and brings the issue to His attention:

> *Jesus' mother said to him, "They have no more*
> *wine." "Woman, why do you involve me?" Jesus*
> *replied. "My hour has not yet come." (John*
> *2:3–4)*

It sounds like a snub: the distant "woman", the cold "why do you involve me?" Various English translations say, "You must not tell me what to do." Once again, it is an indication of the fact that Jesus creates space between His mother and Himself. He is no longer a little boy. The relationships are changing, which takes getting used to, especially for Mary.

The next time, Jesus is teaching in a crowded house. His mother and brothers are outside and ask whether they can speak with Him. Jesus is alerted to his family's request, and He says, "Who is my mother, and who are my brothers?" (Matthew 12:48)

It may not even seem that strange to learn that His brothers were not followers of Jesus, but in the Gospels they seem to feel some lack of understanding of (or even antipathy towards) Jesus. It isn't until Acts that we see James, brother of Jesus, convert and act as a leader of the believers in Jerusalem.

Even from the cross, while lovingly caring for His mother – Jesus keeps his distance from Mary:

> *When Jesus saw his mother there, and the*
> *disciple whom he loved standing nearby, he said*
> *to her, "Woman, here is your son" (John 19:26)*

Why is Jesus so distant to his family? He demonstrates an important paradox of life: God opens your life to relationships, but the relationship with God takes up so much space that, if you wish to maintain that relationship properly, all other relationships will have to yield. Jesus keeps creating space in the circle of primary family relationships, because those relationships keep Him away from that one, true relationship that everything is about. Based on His primary relationship with His Father, Jesus formed relationships with people that sent God His way. Henri Nouwen summarized: "Jesus was often forced to say no to his family, to be able to say yes to his heavenly Father."

Creating space in relationships

Men, do you want to do what God asks of you and love your wife? Truly love her? If so, then leave your father and mother. Don't live your life in response to your parents' expectations. Don't live your life in response to your "father wound". Live the life that God has planned for you. Make space in your immediate family relationships. This creation of space is exactly the thought behind these shocking, radical passages:

> *Anyone who loves their father or mother more than me is not worthy of me; anyone who loves their son or daughter more than me is not worthy of me. (Matthew 10:37)*

> *If anyone comes to me and does not hate father and mother, wife and children, brothers and sisters – yes, even their own life – such a person cannot be my disciple. (Luke 14:26)*

The first text is limited to family relationships. The second text also involves the partner of the man: even in your relationship with your wife, you must create the necessary space so that you can first and foremost maintain a relationship with God, have yourself directed by Him, so that, based on your relationship with Him, you can serve and love your wife as you are supposed to. The Genesis principle ("That is why a man will leave his father and shall unite to his wife") somewhat conflicts with Jesus' call to shape your relationship with Him first. Jesus isolates the disciple. He turns him into a loner, and only after developing a new, primary, transcendent relationship with the Father can life can be properly lived. The radical call to follow is not a call for a Jihad-like life. It is an invitation to be part of a boisterous, intimate love relationship with the Father.

Jesus is good, but not safe

I (Theo) have remarkable parents. I feel very loved. For the past 31 years, they have been praying for me on a daily basis. My ability to love and to receive love is something I have them to thank for. I take that loving nature with me into the world, and for that I am very grateful to them. But there's much more that I learned at home, just like anyone else: unwritten values and standards, expectations and assignments. Live responsibly. Be careful. Thoroughly motivate your decisions. Good is safe. Safe is good. These are great standards to live by, which encourage you to constantly develop yourself as a person. At the same time, I discovered how important it is to be aware of their influence, because they can also have an inhibiting effect.

Five years ago, out of the blue, Henk told me: "Being good at what you do is important to you. You need to be the best player on your team, don't you?" Ouch! I didn't let him see it back then, but his comment struck a sensitive chord in me. And to make matters worse, he topped it with a question: "When was the last time that you messed up at something?" Silence. I realized that I hardly ever messed up. After all, "Safe is good. Good is safe." "No idea, Henk," I had to reluctantly admit.

This was the first time that I became aware of how the influences of your home situation affect your attitude towards life, how you deal with people and approach certain situations. Those influences are both encouraging and inhibiting. In addition, I became more aware of the impact of parents on how you see God and on your interactions with the Heavenly Father. In order to realize a deeper passion and more intimacy in my relationship with God, I noticed that I needed to learn how to live with life-affirming blamelessness as Psalm 84:11 suggests. Based on my background, I also tried to do this in life with God, at the risk of often feeling that I wasn't doing enough, or that what I was doing wasn't good enough. I was happy with my new-found awareness, because it allowed me to make some changes in my life.

This insight into my own story, into what I have picked up in my childhood and youth, helped me to grow in terms of grace, open-mindedness, impulsiveness, primary responses, and spontaneous actions, in daily life and in my interactions with God. I am happy with this development. After all, Jesus sometimes asks us to do radically impossible, and impossibly radical, things. And in these situations, we often have little time to think. "Feed them. Get out of your boat. Stay awake and pray. Forgive seventy times seven times." Jesus is good, but He is not always safe. He can sometimes be life-threatening. Sometimes, you don't only have to throw yourself overboard, but also everything you've learned. Your desire for accuracy, carefulness, rationality, safety – these are all traits that we feel are good to have… traits that come across as examples of wise stewardship and responsible faith. But, they are not a response to what Jesus asks of us; He sometimes asks for more than we were taught at home (as valuable as those lessons may be). I sometimes just have to close my eyes, let go of the brakes, and ignore my brain in order to be able to live primarily for the Heavenly Father and to live the life that He has planned for me.

I want you

Jesus gave the relationship with His Father absolute priority, because He knew how His Father felt about Him. In the monumental prologue of his book, John the Evangelist tells us where Jesus was before He came to live among men: in the "bosom of the Father". This instantly evokes the image of a child sitting on his father's lap, but that's not what John meant. It is more like the image of two people who were lying down before a meal (as was customary in Jesus' era) and are strongly focused on each other, making eye contact, having an intimate heart-to-heart conversation. Where was the Son before He joined us? In the immediate vicinity of His Father. He lived at the heart of God the Father in passionate love, in intimate communion and communication with Him. He lived with God until He came to earth, which changed Him dramatically. But, Jesus did not lose His sensitivity for the things of His Father. Even as a 12-year-old boy, He was aware of the fact that the house of His Father was the best place on earth. Jesus, the son of carpenter Joseph, was not just any ordinary Jewish boy. Nobody had ever seen God, and this young boy was talking about "My Father". This was someone who "had been there". Jesus knew the Father in person and longed to be a voice for the heart of His Father among the people of his time. That was His bigger cause. He was a man on a mission. But even before He had preached one sentence, before He had performed a single miracle, there was the baptism, the dove, the opened heaven, and... the voice: "You are my Son, whom I love; with you I am well pleased." (Luke 3:22)

Before anything else, there is the voice of the Father, the voice telling the Son who He is: the Loved One. The Father emphasizes how unique the relationship is between the two of them. "You are my Son, on you I lay my calling, my anointing rests upon you, my love is for you." That is the beginning. Jesus roamed the world, knowing that God loved Him intensely. *The Favoured One.* This allowed Him to live the way He lived. This was His secret.

And it didn't stop there. Three times during Jesus' life on earth, a voice sounded from heaven, each time confirming that the Father's love goes out to His Son. This same awareness may also seep through as the foundation of our own existence. Before everything I do, before any of my performances, before I do my very best, there is God's voice, telling me: "I love you, my son." It brings the awareness:

He.

Wants.

Me.

Chances are that you need to hear this often. We need to constantly be reminded of the basic truth about our lives: that we are intensely loved by the Father.

Joey

Across the street from me (Henk) lives an eight-year-old boy named Joey. Joey looks a little like a small version of Wayne Rooney. He is what you'd call a true Joey: sassy face, crew-cut hair, earring, teeth that have enough room in between them to park your bike, and always up to no good. Mothers frequently ring Joey's doorbell to complain that Joey has beaten up their son.

Joey lives at home with his mother and his two older sisters. His father ran off this past Christmas. In addition to the people living there, the house also offers a home to two dogs – fighting dogs. Whenever those dogs are being walked, I always keep a close eye on my daughters.

Humanly speaking, Joey faces all the ingredients of a difficult life. Ruth and I refuse to accept that, and we include Joey and his family in our prayers. However, we didn't always talk much to Joey and his mum. A couple of months ago, however, things started to change. It all started with the charity run for the elementary school that both our oldest daughter Manoa and Joey attend. They had plotted a track, and the youngest kids got to run first. Dozens of parents were loudly cheering on their kids. With my son Chris in the stroller and my daughter Emma's hand in mine, I joined Manoa for one round. It was great fun.

After the youngest grades, it was the turn of Joey's class. I looked around, and I didn't see anybody there to cheer Joey on. No father. No mother. However, Joey was very committed and ran through the field. As he passed me, I cheered him on: "Go, Joey, go, Joey! You're doing a great job." Joey heard his name being chanted and looked up in sheer wonder. To the sky. Who was calling his name? Who was cheering him on? With renewed strength, he kept running. Soon, he came around the corner again, and I started chanting again: "Go, Joey!" And again, he looked at the bright and cloudy sky, gloriously confused. It was that miraculous voice again, the voice from heaven.

A couple of days later, I told our girls: "Let's give Joey all of our gogos." (Gogos are plastic figurines that were handed out as collectibles at the grocery store.) Manoa and Emma had only been interested in the golden gogos – as princesses are – and we kept the rest of the figurines in a big box. It made the girls a little nervous to visit Joey's house, but they joined me anyway. We rang the doorbell. One of Joey's sisters opened the door. His mum was watching from the living room. At our request, they called Joey down, and we gave him our gogos. He didn't know what hit him. So many gogos! All for him!

A couple of weeks later, we went away on holiday. Never before had we packed our car as carefully as we did this time. Bicycles on the roof, trailer good to go; nothing could go wrong. At 2 p.m. we loaded our children into the car. I got behind the wheel and turned the key. Nothing. I felt my blood start to boil, and I tried again. Nothing. That was when Joey's mum came outside with her kids. Ever since the "voice from heaven" and the gogos, our relationship with them had greatly improved, but we had never truly talked to Joey's mum. She saw me breaking a sweat, trying to get the car going. She thought it was interesting and stopped to watch, and then she and Ruth started to talk. It would prove to be a beautiful and deep conversation, a conversation in which Joey's mum explained that – ever since his father left – Joey never sleeps in his own bed, but spends the nights in the basket with the fighting dogs or in his sisters' or mum's room.

Meanwhile, I had called the breakdown services. When

the conversation was over, another neighbour approached me. She is a very religious woman, a sister from our church. She said, "Henk, this may sound strange, but I think you should start the car again. I think all of this had to happen for you to build a connection with Joey's mum. Please, get in the car and try again."

Well, what choice did I have? I am a pastor. If there's anyone who should have faith, it is me. Obediently, I got back in the car, although I felt a little silly. I turned the key... and...

Well, to cut a long story short, the breakdown mechanic did a great job helping us get that car started.

Resting at God's heart

Relationship. It all started with a voice from heaven. God sees more in you than just a superhero, someone who is able to make a difference in the world. There is a deeper layer underneath – accepting your responsibilities in church and accepting challenges for the Lord. Jesus invites you to be one with Him in a very intimate way. This is not usually a very easy invitation for men to accept. It has always been like that. Take Adam, for instance. When he had sinned, he decided to hide from God. That is how men work. We play hide-and-seek. But God found him. What do you think His first words were? "Adam, come here. You've made a mess, and you're the one who is going to have to fix it"? No. God's voice said, "Adam, where are you? I want you."

Why would you hide your heart from the loving call of God? Are you ashamed? Did you never let the invitation reach your heart? Or are you stuck in the world of rationality? Does it feel uncomfortable to see yourself as a loved one of the Beloved?

Everything other than living in intimacy with the Father makes Christianity a mechanical entity, a set of dry bones. A.W. Tozer says:

> The outlook on life of the human race will
> change once every person is able to believe that
> we live under a friendly heaven and that God,
> although exalted in power and majesty, longs for
> our friendship.

Do you believe that God passionately longs for your friendship?

Praying in the third person singular

David was someone who believed this with his heart and soul. He was a warrior, but he was also a poet. He had mastered both the sword and the harp. His muscles were hardened, but his heart was soft and alive – for God. But, just like any other man, David had the father wound. However, he discovered that by having a sense of intimacy with the Heavenly Father, the wound can heal and the pain can go away. He said:

> You make known to me the path of life; you will
> fill me with joy in your presence, with eternal
> pleasures at your right hand. (Psalm 16:11)

Based on his intimacy with God, David was able to show his parents mercy and was able to maintain integrity in a world full of hostility. From his place at the side of the Father, David was able to find the right balance between his own dreams and those of God, and he was capable of distinguishing his pure motives from his double motives. This was strikingly expressed in David's response to a *no* from God. One night, David had a dream, which, so far as we are able to see, was one that came from a pure motive: he wanted to build a temple for God. Why would that be a bad plan? David couldn't handle the fact that he lived in a house that was more beautiful than God's house, and he wanted to fix this. Nathan, the prophet, welcomed David's idea. But then, God intervened. He called Nathan to order and instructed him to tell David that God did not (yet) want a temple. In addition, God told him that David's plan was exactly that: David's plan. Not God's plan. God wanted to be the one asking someone to build His temple. He didn't want to accept David's initiative.

How did David respond to God's *no*?

He could have just pursued his will, as so many men do. He could have sacrificed everything to realize his dream, one way or the other. He could have changed into a tyrant. But none of this happened. The primary and most important relationship in David's life was his relationship with God. David had spent enough time at the side of the Father to realize that God wants what's best for him, always, even if he is not able to see it for himself.

When David heard Nathan's message, he retreated into the sanctuary and fell to his knees. He made himself small. The king was on the floor, as a small child on his father's lap. "Who am I?" he prayed. And then, he said something that is perhaps the most impressive thing of all: "What more can David say to you? For you know your servant, Sovereign LORD." (2 Samuel 7:20)

David referred to himself as David in his own prayer. Little children do that with adults. Great men do that with an almighty God.

The Bible says that we, in Christ, "are seated at the right hand of the Father". As David was sitting with God in the sanctuary, so may we sit with our Father. There, in that intimate encounter with Jesus, at the bosom of the Father, is where David's experience can also become ours. This is where the father wound can heal. All of those painful wounds, inflicted by distant, passive, authoritarian, abusive, absent, or accusing fathers, mothers, coaches, teachers, or other authority figures, are healed there. Once we have found that place, the heart of the Father, the voice will become increasingly clear and will touch our soul more deeply: *You are my beloved Son, in whom I am well pleased.*

The great man becomes a little boy, and with that, the little boy in us becomes a great man. It is this paradox that relieves the boy of his hessian sack, allowing him to see the eagle.

4

Prepared to die

*"D'Artagnan! D'Artagnan!" cried she, "is it you?
This way! this way!"*

*"Constance? Constance?" replied the young
man, "Where are you? Where are you? My God!"*

*At the same moment the door of the cell
yielded to a shock, rather than opened; several
men rushed into the chamber. Mme. Bonacieux
had sunk into an armchair, without the power of
moving.*

*D'Artagnan threw down a yet-smoking pistol
which he held in his hand, and fell on his knees
before his mistress. Athos replaced his in his
belt; Porthos and Aramis, who held their drawn
swords in their hands, returned them to their
scabbards.*

*"Oh, d'Artagnan, my beloved d'Artagnan! You
have come, then, at last! You have not deceived
me! It is indeed thee!"*

"Yes, yes, Constance. Reunited!"

ALEXANDRE DUMAS

So, what exactly went wrong in the fall of man? The woman was seduced by the snake and took a fruit from the tree of knowledge of good and evil. She took a bite from the fruit, and the damage was done. It seems as if the question of who is to blame for the fall of man points primarily to the woman. And for centuries, the actions of Eve have been cited as evidence to prove the alleged wickedness of the woman. But where was Adam, the man, in this instance?

This question instantly summarizes the entire problem: Where was Adam? He was somewhere, obviously, but not where he should have been. In Genesis 2:15, God commissions the man to "work and take care of" the Garden of Eden. The Hebrew word that was translated to "take care of" could also be translated as "guard", as has been done in certain Bible translations. The task of the man was to cultivate and guard the Garden of Eden. But guard it against what, exactly? There were no such things as hostile tribes yet. Adam didn't even have a wife yet. However, the power of darkness did already exist at that time. In addition, animals were classified as "tame cattle", "birds", and "wild animals". God had also given the man the task of guarding the garden against "the animals of the field", the wild animals that did not live in the garden.

Somewhere, Adam must have had a hole in his defences, because one of the wild animals, the snake, finds its way into the garden. Somewhere, Adam has messed up, was negligent. And it doesn't stop there.

After Eve has spoken to the snake and has taken a bite from the apple, she gives the remainder of the fruit to the man "who was with her". So, while the snake was seducing his wife, Adam was with her the whole time. And he said nothing.

The sin of negligence

What we see here is the core of the problem that many men have. Outdoors, we are strong, are able to move mountains, but we fail to care for our garden. We allow holes in our defence system. Poisonous vipers invade our houses and spray their deadly venom. We watch as our women struggle, flounder, and lose themselves. We say nothing as our children lose their way and slide towards the abyss. And yes, we can blame a lot of people for everything that goes wrong, but it all started with the question: Where was Adam? Not where he should have been, that's for sure.

He walked through the darkness.

He just stood there and watched.

He was silent when he should have spoken up.

And when God called him to account, Adam blamed his wife.

Negligence is a sin. In the parable of the talents, there is only one who is "thrown into the outer darkness". It isn't the men who took risks. No. It's that one man who did nothing. Apathy is what infuriates God. Too many men live like an ostrich, sticking their head in the sand when danger lurks. We spend too much of our lives in the fast lane to notice what is going on, and by the time we finally stop, it is too late.

An annoying Bible passage

I can't begin to count the times that I have read Ephesians 5:21–33 with a soon-to-be husband and wife during their marriage preparation: that section in which the woman is called to be submissive to her husband, and the man is told to love his wife. Often, I have noticed that this passage provokes significant resistance from women. Being submissive? That is so outdated! Haven't we established in our postmodern society that men and women are equals? The man usually sits there and says nothing. As if to imply: "I don't agree with that section, honey, but please calm down. This is just a marriage preparation session."

I am amazed as much by the response of the man as by the woman. Because, if there's anyone who should respond defensively during that section, it's the man! The woman is told to be submissive to her husband. *Big deal!* Because the previous verse says, "Submit to one another out of reverence for Christ."

Everyone. Each other. Woman, be submissive to other women. Men, be submissive to other men. Men, be submissive to your wife. Women, be submissive to your husband. When, in verse 22, Paul says that the woman must be submissive to her husband "as to the Lord", he is, in fact, not saying anything new.

And it gets even more interesting, if you realize that some Greek translations say: "Women, to your husband as to the Lord."

See which word is missing? (Our advice is not to tell your wife. It could lead to undesirable situations in future marital disputes. Just when you try to silence her with the biblical truth, "You have to listen to me, because the Bible says that you must be submissive to me!" she can slap you with "Then show me where it says so in Greek." And, before you know it, you're throwing various Greek manuscripts at each other, and you're being arrested for domestic violence.)

The sentence in verse 22 continues in the spirit of verse 21: "Be submissive to one another out of respect for what Jesus did, everyone to everyone – and women, this also applies to you in your relationship with your husband."

The reason for being submissive to one another lies in what Jesus did for us. The Son of God gave His life for us, and in doing so, told us all: This is how valuable you are! This is what God is willing to sacrifice for you!

Out of respect for Jesus

When Revd David Wilkerson travelled from his rural home town to New York in 1958 to preach the gospel to the members of violent youth gangs, he reached out to Nicky Cruz, the leader of the feared Mau-Mau gang. Nicky didn't want anything to do with David Wilkerson, but the skinny minister continued to visit him. During one of these visits, Nicky slapped him in the face, spat at him, and threatened to kill him. David simply persevered in saying that Jesus loved Nicky. A couple of days later, Reverend Wilkerson visited Nicky again, and said:

> *Nicky, you can stab me to death. You can chop me up and scatter the pieces across the street. But still, every piece of me will tell you: "Jesus loves you."*

Nicky eventually became a believer, as did many other members of the gang. Who is able to resist unconditional love? Jesus loved us. He gave His life for the Nickys, Joeys, and Rudys of this world. He gave His life for you and for me. And His exceptional act of love makes every human being valuable. The fact that the Son of God gave His life for the cashier at the supermarket, for the neighbour down the street, and for my colleagues at work tells me that I must treat them with the utmost respect. This awareness must have a central place in my attitude towards any person: after all, Jesus thought that this person was worth dying for. *Be submissive to one another. Out of respect for Jesus.* And, arising from that principle, women should also be submissive to their husbands. This isn't something extraordinary. The assignment for women is to consider their husbands to be at least equally as valuable as all other people. The fact is, we men often give our wives enough reasons to doubt our value. Perhaps that is why the Bible gives women an extra incentive to accept the authority of her husband.

The true challenge

So, the call for the woman is not something to get upset about, unless you already have trouble dealing with Jesus' love for people in general and you in particular. The true challenge in Ephesians 5 does not concern the woman, but the man: "Husbands, love your wives, just as Christ loved the church and gave himself up for her."

Whereas the man must be as submissive to his wife as his wife is to him, he has another, bigger assignment: love your wife. However, "loving" exists in many shapes and sizes. How should men love their wives? "Just as Christ loved the church and gave himself up for her." That's how. Be prepared to give your own life for that of your wife.

Your wife is worth dying for.

Does she know that you feel that way about her?

What would happen to your wife if every bone in her body were convinced of the fact that – should the circumstance arise – you would give your life for her, without hesitation, instantly, because she is so valuable and special to you. And what would happen to your wife if, until the day you actually get the chance to die for her, you show her every day, through countless little things, that she is the one who lights up your life?

I (Henk) am not a fighter by nature. However, I did fight once. Well, almost. With a really tall Greek man, who had a very thick moustache. I remember the details of that moustache very well, because it made a big impression on me. We were on a jeep safari in the mountains with a group of Dutchmen, supervised by the tall Greek. Ruth was driving the front jeep, and I was driving the rear one. On a steep section, the engine of Ruth's car failed. She tried to drive to the top using the Ramp Test, but she wasn't able to. She was trying so hard that the engine started to smoke. The tall Greek saw that his jeep was in trouble, and he walked towards Ruth's jeep. Instead of helping her, he started yelling at her. With his big Greek moustache, inches away from my wife, who was trying so hard.

I got out of my car and rushed towards the tall Greek. And I almost fought him. I didn't care that he thought that Ruth should have treated his jeep differently. Nobody yells at my wife like that. Nobody.

Eventually, I saw a sparkle in his eyes. I think he appreciated the fact that I was willing to punch his unshaven face out of love for my wife. Greeks love that kind of thing. Although, I must add that I had threatened to tell his boss how rude his employee was to female customers. Be that as it may, after his sincere apologies, I was able to put my fists down.

And Ruth? Whoa! Boy, did she show me how much women love the fact that you are willing to give your life for them. Or at least, are willing to fight for them with a tall Greek who smells like olives and garlic.

***

I (Theo) can relate, although the Greek that I almost fought because I thought he was calling my wife all kinds of names had no moustache. Oh, and there is another difference. The fist I would have wanted to swing at him would have been completely unfair. I'll explain.

Harmke (my wife) and I lived and worked in the Greek city of Thessaloniki for a while. In general, life among the Greeks was good. They are not always very friendly, but they are incredibly sociable nonetheless.

One day, I got a call at the office. It was Harmke. She sounded very unhappy. Her car had broken down in front of a traffic light, and the engine was smoking (later it would appear that the fan belt had snapped). The problem was that she couldn't move the car anywhere that was safe in the narrow streets of Thessaloniki. The crowded traffic was trying to make its way past our car, and drivers were aggressively honking at her. Although the Greek sky is usually sunny and blue, it was remarkably rainy, wet, and cold that day. After receiving a call like that, a man feels his adrenaline start to pump, and so I tried to reach Harmke as quickly as possible with the help of Gregoris, a Greek colleague. When we finally arrived, she was waiting outside on the kerb in the pouring rain. To make matters worse, she told me that a Greek man had continually been screaming and yelling at her from across the street while making angry gestures. Before she could finish telling me her story, I was already rushing towards him. I was ready to tell him that it's fine for him to be upset about a traffic jam, but that yelling at my wife is not OK. In my best Greek, I angrily asked him what his problem was. I don't think I did a good job, because Gregoris quickly took over. And then, Gregoris started laughing. I wasn't sure if I shared his sense of humour, until he said: "Do you know what he has been trying to tell Harmke? 'Quickly, come over to my store. It's warm and dry in here. You don't have to be in the rain. Just stay here until you find help.'"

This situation taught me several important lessons. Lesson one: "Complete your language course before moving abroad." Lesson two: "Know the culture. Understand that a Greek talks with his hands and can't speak without yelling." And lesson three: "Try to find more opportunities to get yourself into these kinds of situations, because your wife will love it when you stick up for her."

By the way, Henk and I would like to mention that both of our women are much better drivers than we are (and yes, we wrote this sentence without any form of coercion).

Once your wife knows that you think she is worth dying for, you're no longer talking about trivial matters, such as who runs the house. These are things that are only discussed by couples who don't get it. Who runs our homes? Ruth and Harmke both know that we will never sacrifice their happiness or that of our children for our ambitions. And Ruth and Harmke want us to realize and achieve our dreams. And you may frequently face difficult questions, such as: What direction should we take with our family? But, if your relationship is based on sacrificial love and mutual submissiveness, you'll be able to find unanimous solutions to difficult issues.

Love that increases beauty

The kind of love that Christ had for his church is called *agape* in Greek. Men, love your wives, as Christ has "*agape*-d" the church. *Agape* is also used in that extremely popular Bible verse, John 3:16: "because God has '*agape*-d' the world so intensely, that he has given his Son." *Agape* is the highest, most noble form of love. *Agape* means being prepared to die for the object of one's affection.

And the best thing is: *agape* always makes the other more beautiful. The verses in Ephesians 5 explain what Christ's love did for His church: His love has cleansed the church and made it radiant, without spots or wrinkles. His love has made the church holy and immaculate. *Agape* love allows the other to shine, makes the other pure, and brings out hidden beauty. *Agape* doesn't love people because they are beautiful or special. *Agape makes* them beautiful and special.

Men, love your wives in such a way that she keeps growing more beautiful!

When looking at a woman, you can tell whether her husband loves her. You can see it in her eyes. When women are "*agape*-d" by their husband, their eyes shine and the woman herself glows. The beloved woman radiates an enchantment of love, so intense that everyone around her gets a little something of that love too.

That is our own story as well. God's *agape* love has made us beautiful. Jesus died for us when we were sinners, enemies of God. He came to us as we were drowning in a smelly swamp of sin, and He pulled us from our cesspool of corruption and washed us. He cleansed us. His love made us lovable. His *agape* made us pure. His grace made us desirable, courageous, human.

Agape transforms people into the people they are meant to be.

Imagine having a wife who is constantly disappointing you. She doesn't want the same things that you want; she is cynical, critical, petulant, and always has something to complain about. What would happen if you were to get up tomorrow with the intention of *"agape*-ing" her — if you were to encourage her, tell her how beautiful she is, open the door for her, and spoil her with her favourite magazine? What would that do to your wife? You would wake her up with a kiss. She would think: "What's happened to my husband? This is great! I'd better change my attitude, so that he keeps this up!"

Gradually, she would start to believe what you're saying. More and more, she would behave the way she knows is loved and desired by you. In the previous chapter, we saw how the Father began by expressing love for His Son, even before He had done anything. The love of His Father made Jesus who He was. The love of Jesus for His disciples made them into what they were in the end. Love enables people to live up to their potential.

Questions that the bus girl should have asked

Some men have "had" a lot of women, and they brag about it. They think that all of their "conquests" allow them to demonstrate how strong and how brave they are. The sad part is that the only thing these men actually demonstrate is how pathetic and how cowardly they are. They are too weak to remain loyal to one woman. They are too cowardly to give their life for one partner. And because they are not brave enough or strong enough to give one woman what she deserves, they seek refuge in countless quick escapades, so that they can fool themselves and their peers with a surrogate of love, strength, and courage.

One time, I (Henk) was riding on the bus, and there was a young couple sitting behind me. They were still children, about 14 or 15 years old. And these children were telling each other what they were planning to do to one another once they arrived at her room. I got a little hot under the collar, as they were really planning to do a lot!

What would it be like if the bus girl, instead of planning to engage in all of these things with the bus boy, would instead ask him first: "Who are you, really? What are you like? Are you strong? Are you courageous? Would you dare to fight for me? Do you have the strength to stay loyal to me? Do you think I'm worth giving your life for?" And what if she would only do all of these things with the bus boy after being completely convinced of the boy's positive answers to her questions? If this were the case, the bus boy would have long since outgrown his boyhood. Because, in order to find the answers to these big questions, you first need to develop several years' worth of maturity. The bus boy would have to become a man. And this new man would promise the bus girl, in the presence of all of her family and friends, that he is indeed strong enough to stay faithful to her forever, and that he is courageous enough to die for her. They would form an alliance of marriage. And from the protection of that alliance, they would be able to engage in all of those activities that they had been planning that one afternoon on the bus. Only now, all of those things would not be an expression of a quest for something they were both longing for. Instead, they would be a celebration of what they had found in one another!

When you *agape* your wife, you won't find any snakes in your garden. Take your assignment to make your garden beautiful and to protect it extremely seriously. Don't spend your evenings apathetically in front of the television or with your favourite hobby. With active involvement, you can take the initiative to build your home and to protect your family. From your primary relationship with the Heavenly Father, you can surprise your wife with love, make her beauty emerge like a young flower, and show her the mysteries of life. Maybe it is time to confess your sin of negligence and ask God to lead you down the road of *agape*-ing your wife.

5

I make you my king

*They walked arm in arm, occupying the whole
width of the street and taking in every Musketeer
they met, so that in the end it became a
triumphal march. The heart of d'Artagnan swam
in delirium; he marched between Athos and
Porthos, pressing them tenderly.*

ALEXANDRE DUMAS

Friendship. I don't know anyone who doesn't long for
it. And yet, I only know a few men who actually have it.
People sometimes say, "Women have friends. Men have
colleagues." Some men turn their colleagues into friends,
but true friendship among men is rare. That is tragic.
Because friendship is not only "beautiful" and "important":
friendship is vital. Yes, it is important to create space in
your primary relationships, allowing you to give your first
and biggest loyalty to God. But, at the same time, you need
to allow men into your life and give God the opportunity to
lead you and bless you through male friends.

Friendship is a spiritual discipline... just as important
as praying, Bible reading, or giving. Countless men have
lost friendships in the quest of pursuing a career. Other
men want to pursue friendships, but instead they act like

hedgehogs. Still, the power of friendship is extraordinary.

David was facing a difficult period in his life. After his victory over Goliath, he ended up in Saul's court and received an important position in his army. He grew popular... too popular. Saul became jealous of David and wanted to get rid of him. It took six (failed) murder attempts to chase David into the desert. He would roam there for ten years, as hunted game. Ten years of pursuit by a mad king. For ten years, the promise of God – "You will be the new king" – was not fulfilled. Ten years of living as a refugee. Imagine what it would take to stay loyal to God, and to yourself, in this situation. Hundreds of times, David had more than enough reason to become dejected, to take matters into his own hands, and to violently take what God had promised him long ago. But David waited, ran, believed. Twice, Saul was at his mercy, but David refused to seize the opportunity. We see him struggling in the desert, struggling with God and with himself, with internal and external enemies. But he won. He emerged stronger, glowing with the Spirit, strong in his faith, ready for the real deal.

How is that possible? What did David have that Saul did not have? Saul started out good, just like David. In the Bible, we read that, at the beginning of his reign, Saul was "captivated by the Spirit" and "was given a new heart" by God. In addition, Saul had many qualities that were required to be a great king: he was strong, courageous, resourceful, and had faith. He started out good, but he ended his life as a bitter and jealous old man. Where did things go wrong with Saul?

Saul was always alone. He had no friends, no circle of heroes, no *band of brothers.* Throughout the Saul story, we see a lonely Saul, who makes his own decisions, who processes his own grief, who fights his own battles. No counsellors, no confidants, no friends.

The biggest friendship story from the Bible

David shared many of the same traits that Saul had: a new heart, the Spirit of God, courage, resourcefulness, faith. However, there was one big difference: David had a friend. And not just any friend. The most beautiful and touching friendship from the Bible was the one between David and Jonathan. Their friendship was formed when David was still a rookie. He was like d'Artagnan, one day in Paris. Snatched away from the sheep, he was anointed as the new king. Once in a while, he could play his harp for the king, and in one great moment, he snapped at Goliath. He was a shepherd with a sling, a hairy robe, and a harp. He could sing, play, and sling. He had his wounds and his dreams. As an 18-year-old, he struck down Goliath. Saul was impressed and invited him to the palace. Jonathan, Saul's son and his envisioned successor, was present. Jonathan was an experienced warrior; 30 years old, in the prime of his life. His courage and his martial arts skills were legendary. Jonathan was like Brad Pitt in the portrayal of Achilles, the Greek hero who defeated Hercules in the battle of Troy. The renowned warrior and the young, religious shepherd. They became one. The Bible states it as follows:

> *Jonathan became one in spirit with David, and he loved him as himself.... And Jonathan made a covenant with David because he loved him as himself. Jonathan took off the robe he was wearing and gave it to David, along with his tunic, and even his sword, his bow and his belt. (1 Samuel 18:1, 3–4)*

Not long after entering into their bond of friendship, David had to flee into the desert. His ten desert years began with friendship. And they ended with it. In 2 Samuel 1:25, 26, David sang for his deceased friend, Jonathan:

> *How the mighty have fallen in battle! Jonathan lies slain on your heights.*
> *I grieve for you, Jonathan my brother; you were very dear to me. Your love for me was wonderful, more wonderful than that of women.*

In all those years of despair, confusion, and conflict, there was always one ray of hope, one person who kept him human, one friend who didn't allow him to forget that God is love. In a world that was nothing but hostile, where survival of the fittest was law, Jonathan reminded David of the fact that love, friendship, and peace exist... that God is loyal, and He has not forgotten about His promise that there are things in life that are worth holding on for.

What was striking about the friendship between Jonathan and David was that it seemed to be one-sided: Jonathan gave; David received. Jonathan felt an instant attraction to David. Jonathan felt an intense friendship towards him. Jonathan loved David as much as his own life. Jonathan befriended David. Jonathan gave – his robe, his armour. Jonathan was the elder of the two men. He was 12 years older than David, used to the etiquette and intrigues of the court, and hardened by life.

In this period of his life, David was not in a position to give much. Materially speaking, he hardly owned anything: a sling and a shepherd bag, that was all. In terms of life experience, he was still wet behind the ears. His network consisted mostly of sheep, along with some lions and a bear.

David only had David. With all of his wounds, dreams, and expectations. With his big secret: "I have been anointed." And later, with all the pressure of surviving in the desert. The only thing David had to give was his wounded, confused, religious self, and that was enough for Jonathan. More than enough.

"You are my king"

Jonathan gave. In the text that describes how their friendship was formed, we see Jonathan give David three things: a promise, his robe, and his armour. In fact, Jonathan tells David: "I make you my king. I acknowledge God's anointing on your life. You are special, and I value you." Imagine what this must have meant to David. It was the first time that anyone had ever looked past his exterior. Nobody had ever treated him like what he felt he was worth. And then there was Jonathan. He made a covenant with David: "We belong together. We will stay loyal to one another." Jonathan's soul became linked to David's. They visited each other's homes. As a broken bone grows back together while healing, their lives became bonded.

From this moment on, David had a confidant at the court. He had a friend in high places. Through Jonathan, he had direct access to the king. This didn't make life any easier for Jonathan; it was actually quite the opposite. In the years that followed, Jonathan continually had to navigate between his loyalty to his father and his covenant with his friend. Throughout all of this, we never see Jonathan waver. He remains loyal to both David and his father. He keeps visiting David, even in the desert. He will die at the side of his father, in the battle against the Philistines. Jonathan was prepared to proceed on the road less travelled: the road of friendship.

The second thing Jonathan gave to David was his robe. That may just seem like a nice thing to do, such as: "Jonathan gave David his coat." However, it was actually a much bigger gesture made by Jonathan towards David. Back then, a robe was a big deal. During his lifetime, a man usually received just one robe, often from his father. This robe symbolized his manhood. And more. The robe was an earthly representation of a heavenly plan. The Hebrew word for robe is *addereth* and means "glory, great, grand, robe". The robe symbolized the greatness of a person. When Joseph's father Jacob gave him a robe that was bigger and more beautiful than that of his brothers, his brothers weren't jealous because he received a cooler jacket than they did. The pain of the older brothers was in the fact that Jacob had assigned their younger brother a greater anointing and a higher position than them. Each priest was given a sacred robe, based on the heavenly example that God showed Moses. Wearing the priest's robe was what visibly made the priest a priest. The anointing of his ministry, the strength and greatness of his profession... all of that was interwoven with the garment. When Elijah gave his robe to Elisha, the value of that was much greater than giving a garment to keep him warm and dry. By giving his robe, Elijah passed on his divine anointment, his prophetic gift, and his greatness to Elisha.

Jonathan had one robe, and he would never get another one. This robe contained his future kingdom, his courage, his character, his greatness as a person, and his divine anointing. He gave all of that to David. By giving David his robe, Jonathan gave David his life.

The third thing Jonathan gave David was his armour. Again, a great gesture. It wasn't as if the Israelite army had an abundance of swords, bows, and shields. A couple of years before the first encounter between Jonathan and David, the entire army of Israel had just two swords: one for Saul and one for Jonathan. The Philistines had negotiated a monopoly on iron forging, and by doing so they had created an unequal situation. The Philistines fought with swords, spears, and chariots. The Israelites had to settle for slings, pitchforks, and one or two lost swords. Only the bravest heroes and best warriors were given a sword. A sword was rare, and it was just as important to a warrior as his wife.

Jonathan gave David his armour, and whereas the armour of King Saul was too big and impractical for David, the armour of Jonathan fitted him perfectly. Apparently, both men had the same stature. In addition to a sword, David was given a bow and a belt. With the bow, David could hit distant targets. The sword allowed him to hit targets that were nearby. The belt kept his armour together and allowed him to fight with more flexibility.

Three gifts. What an unexpected blessing! Jonathan poured himself into David. He lifted David onto his shoulders and said: "You can sit here. You can live and fight from my shoulders. I give you my life, my future, my strength and my most valuable possession." That is friendship. In the years that followed, the friendship of David and Jonathan continued to grow. Jonathan didn't allow David to lose himself or become lonely. He stayed loyal.

Lonely at the top?

People sometimes say, "It's lonely at the top." That's possible. It can indeed be lonely at the top, but often it's because the person at the top has not made room for friendships in his life or has sacrificed friendships along the way on the road to his success. Saul is living proof that it can be lonely at the top. The consequences of that loneliness are generally disastrous. David and Jonathan, however, show that you can also have great friends at the top and that you can walk together.

A couple of years ago, I (Henk) felt lonely at my top. I was continually giving lectures, supervising, progressing. Gradually, all of my friendships faded into the background. I supervised Athletes in Action and was the pastor in a church. I thought that loneliness was part of the job until I shared my sense of loneliness with a group of men. Pieter Cnossen, one of the co-founders of The 4th Musketeer, and also a dear friend, came to me and said: "I'll make sure that you're not lonely. I will be your friend." He lived up to his promise. Time after time, he visited me, helped me with chores in my house, or took me places. He gave himself. God gave me a friend. When, years later, Pieter and his wife Hanna tragically lost their firstborn, Joas, I was given the opportunity to be a friend to Pieter. I visited Pieter and Hanna the same day. We prayed together, cried together, talked together. Pieter and Hanna asked me to lead the private funeral service, and together we said goodbye to Joas. There was a time when I was the main recipient of Pieter's friendship, and years later, I was given the opportunity to be his friend.

To whom can I give my friendship?

That's how life works. There is a time of receiving and a time of giving. And there was a time for David to give as well. About 15 years after he first formed a friendship with Jonathan, David was at the peak of his power. Saul and Jonathan had passed away. David had ruled in Jerusalem, steered Israel into calm waters, dealt with the Philistines from time to time, and could now focus on giving. The time of fleeing and fighting was over. God had now given him the chance to rest and opportunities to share. In 2 Samuel 9:1, we suddenly see David ask the same question twice: "Is there anyone still left of the house of Saul to whom I can show kindness for Jonathan's sake?"

What a beautiful question! Is there anyone to whom I can show kindness? Is there anyone left to whom I can be a friend? Critics would say: "A little too late. David should have thought about this sooner." They have a point. But, better late than never. Far too many people never reach this point in life. Did you ever ask yourself this question: "To whom could I show kindness?"

At the table of the king, nobody sees that you're crippled

It turns out that one more descendant of Saul was still alive: Mephibosheth, a son of Jonathan. The Bible gives some significant information about this man: Mephibosheth was crippled in both legs. When his father Jonathan and grandfather Saul were killed by the Philistines, the palace was in panic. The royal household thought that the Philistines were about to invade the castle and murder the entire royal family. His nurse grabbed Mephibosheth – who was five years old at the time – and fled the palace. In her rush, she dropped the boy. He broke both of his legs and, apparently, the fractures didn't heal properly. Mephibosheth would spend the rest of his life as a cripple. Not only were his father and his grandfather dead, but he had also been robbed of his dignity and his ability to live independently. David took possession of the throne of his grandfather, the throne that had been intended for Mephibosheth. If everything had gone according to the rules of royal lineage, Jonathan would have succeeded his father Saul, and Mephibosheth would, in turn, have succeeded Jonathan. But it had all worked out differently, and instead Mephibosheth hid in the desert of Lo-Debar, on the other side of the Jordan. Lo-Debar literally means "infertile soul". That is where Mephibosheth lived. The name of this village represented his life: unfulfilled, infertile, and like a wilted flower... meant to flourish, but faded in the scorching heat of life. Even today, we see crippled people, or people who are disabled in other ways, who are kept from living among the rest. Nobody can see the disabled person. The shame would be too big for the family. That is how Mephibosheth was in the desert: like a dead dog. And then there was his name: Mephibosheth, which, when translated literally, means "seething libel" or "desperate confusion". That was Mephibosheth. Life had not been kind to him. Everything was an endless bad joke. A crippled king's son, hidden in an infertile desert village, where the young man grew up to be a desperate, confused, embittered loner, and where he would spend his endlessly monotonous days, until he slipped away in a miserable death. How sad can a human life be?

But then, there is God, who, through a messenger of David said: "Mephibosheth, the king has found you and he wants to meet you." Agony. His past had caught up with him. Obviously, David wanted to kill him, so that Mephibosheth could never claim his throne. That is how the rules worked back then. That is how they still work today.

But Mephibosheth did not count on David's goodness and the heritage of his father's friendship. It was payback time. When Mephibosheth shrank before the eyes of David, David tried to comfort him: "Don't be afraid." And David gave. He gave Mephibosheth land, cattle, and servants. But above all, he gave Mephibosheth a place at his table. He gave the bitter refugee back his dignity. Mephibosheth's pain was reflected in every fibre of his body, when he whispered in surprise: "Of what importance am I, your servant, that you show regard for a dead dog like me?"

David picked him up and "that is how Mephibosheth was taken in and treated like one of the King's sons at the court". Because there, sitting at the abundant table of the king, nobody could see that he was a cripple. Sitting there, eating at the highest table of the country, he was the equal of the greats on earth.

In what season do you find yourself? Are you under great pressure? Is every day a struggle, and does God seem to endlessly postpone the fulfilment of His promises? Do not wallow in your loneliness, but instead share it with other men. And with God. Open yourself to receive friendship.

Or, has God taken you to a phase in your life during which you can give friendship, where you can find the cripples and the hidden in this world and guide them from their fruitless lives to the table of the King?

The ultimate friend

Maybe you feel like this: "I don't have a friend. How can I ever give friendship?" In that case, don't forget that there is someone who has proven His friendship to you, just like Jonathan proved his friendship to David. We always have Jesus, who said: "You are my friends if you do what I command." (John 15:14)

That is Jesus. He gives us the indescribable privilege of becoming His friends, but it is a different kind of friendship. It is friendship with the One who has all the right in the world to direct us, order us, lead us. He is our King–Friend. In that order.

Jesus has given us His friendship, as Jonathan gave his to David. Just like Jonathan, Jesus made a covenant with us, when he said: "And remember, I am with you each and every day until the end of the age."

He has given us his robe. When Jesus was stripped, nailed to the cross, and crucified for us, He gave us His strength, His dignity, His greatness, and His anointing. And He went way beyond the level of friendship that Jonathan gave to David. He exchanged His dignity for our filth; He gave us His holiness and carried our sin; He injected us with his divine anointing, and He absorbed all of our weakness. He died our death and gave us His life. That is Jesus. "What a friend we have in Jesus", the great nineteenth-century song exalts. He dressed us with His robe and died in our nakedness. He gives His "white clothes, to dress ourselves and to cover our nakedness".

And just like Jonathan gave David his armour, Jesus gives us *spiritual* armour. He gives us a sword, His Word, which allows us to hit nearby targets. By applying the Word in situations close to home, we can give people advice, we can unleash God's strength, and we can bring profound change. Jesus gives us a bow – prayer – with which we can hit targets that are far away. Prayer gives us a global reach. We can hit targets in North Korea, in the Middle East dominated by Islam, and yes, even in heavenly places. Our prayers are like long-range missiles that move heaven and earth to turn problems or emergencies into something good. And finally, Jesus – like Jonathan – gives us a belt: the belt of Truth, which keeps our armour together, allowing us to fight with more flexibility. One of the main effects of sin and lies is that they rob us of our boldness. We start living uncomfortably, we shine less, and we become more inhibited. By staying in God's truth and purity, we can share and give to a maximum extent. Don't let any of your energy drain away into falsehood or sin. Keep your armour intact.

Friendship is the story of giving and receiving, the story of David, Jonathan, and Mephibosheth; the story about Jesus and us; and others. One of the best ways to allow friendship to grow is by going on an adventure together, fighting with the King's army – that unites you in friendship. It gives you something to celebrate and to look back on, something to brag about. Throw your loneliness from your hessian sack and go out on an adventure with other men, with The 4th Musketeer, with your church, or any other way. Pieter, Jan, Theo, and I frequently tell each other: "Later, when we are old and fat, we'll be sitting on a bench together under a tree, and – happy and satisfied with life – we will tell the stories of these adventures that we're experiencing today."

2

ON AN ADVENTURE

Living with Jesus is a process. The journey goes on. We move forward. *More aware* – of the story that we're living. *More honest* – about our deepest motives. *More free and calm* – because of the resonance of the Voice of the Father in the depths of our being. *More powerful* – with a greater ability to love and to build friendships.

It is a wonderful place to be. A wonderful chapter to build in.

And the invitation is always there.

Again, it is a voice from heaven, this time originating from earth: Jesus.

He asks us to participate in a mysterious, global mission, a mission with wondrous dynamics. In our giving, we will receive. By shaping God's intention for us, we ourselves will be shaped to God's purpose.

The adventure to which Jesus invites us is the ideal path on which a boy is given the opportunity to be initiated into manhood. The storms, the challenges, the assignments, the battles – these are not meant to be difficult interruptions in a life that is supposed to be comfortable. They are unimagined opportunities for each of us to be formed into more of a man – by the reality of life, but ultimately by the Father Himself.

This adventure with Jesus is packed with milestones: opportunities to discover what it is that you are dragging along in your hessian sack and chances that will allow your heart to grow. At every single challenge, you'll have the choice to respond either as a boy or as a man. And every single time, the decision we make is relative. Our life is a story. Every time, it appears to be a choice of a direction: the road down, back to less or the climb up, on the way to a greater manhood.

Straight through the storm.

6

To the other side, while sleeping

"Ah, ah!" said Porthos, "it appears there's
something fresh here."
  "Yes, we are going–" said Aramis.
  "To what country?" demanded Porthos....
  "To London, gentlemen," said d'Artagnan....
  "Besides, make yourselves easy; we shall not all
arrive at London."
  "Why so?"
  "Because, in all probability, some one of us will
be left on the road."
  "Is this, then, a campaign upon which we are
now entering?"
  "One of a most dangerous kind, I give you
notice."

ALEXANDRE DUMAS

The global mission to which Jesus invites us has all of the
characteristics of a quest. A quest is a journey to the end of
the world, during which the adventurer has to face the most
amazing hazards. This mission is not a small thing. Lives
are at stake. Courage, perseverance, and accountability are

required. Chances are that you'll be facing opponents of mythical proportions along the way: devils, demons, natural disasters, diseases, attempts at murder. Nobody knows what the journey will be like, and nobody knows the complete route. Some know the next stop. This quest requires unity, loyalty, and sacrifice. Since this concerns real life, with real dangers and a life-saving mission, Jesus trains his friends in the principles of the quest from Day One. In Mark 4:35–41, we witness such a training moment.

To the other side

"At the end of that day." That is how the story begins. It had been a special day, a day packed with inspiring education, divine intervention, and overwhelming miracles. Life simply couldn't get any better than this, or so the disciples believed. They were the friends of Jesus, and they were allowed to share in His fame and power, all in the freedom of their own environment. But the sentence goes on to say: "At the end of that day, when darkness had fallen." It is a first hint at the things that are to come. The glorious day is over, and the darkness of the night takes over.

This is when Jesus proposes one of his creative initiatives – "Let's cross the lake" – because, although the day was over, Jesus' work was far from done. Jesus wanted to cross the lake to the Gadara region, since demons ruled there. He had already seen them, and now the time had come to remove the darkness that covered this area. Thousands of demons had possessed two men. Through these two people, the devils were terrorizing the entire area. No rope, chain, or heavy weapon could do anything against the infernal power of these two men. However, Jesus did not fear the devil. He went for it... across the lake of Galilee. In the perspective of the disciples, that lake was so large that they often called it "the sea". Jesus' friends had an ambivalent attitude towards the lake of Galilee. On one hand, they loved the lake: it provided their livelihood. On the other hand, they — like all other people in Jesus' time — were afraid of the lake. Water was traditionally associated with chaos and the forces of evil. And now, Jesus... in the ominous darkness... Jesus wants to cross the dangerous waters... to the Gadara region, controlled by thousands of demons.

That is a quest.

Make the crossing in the right ship

But, since it was Jesus who asked the disciples to join Him, nobody hesitated and everybody jumped aboard. The Bible says that there were even little boats that accompanied Jesus' ship. Other people from Jesus' circle had heard of His plans to cross and had decided to join Him. Eventually, a massive, deadly storm breaks loose. When — on Jesus' command — everything calms down, we see that only one ship makes it across: Jesus' ship. There is no trace of the other ships. Have they been shipwrecked? Have they fled to a nearby port with heavy damage? Did they go back when they still could? Did people die? We don't know. We do know one thing, though: only one ship makes it across safely.

It is the first important element in a quest: Make sure you are on the right ship, with the right people and the right armour. D'Artagnan begins the dangerous journey to London with his best friends. They know each other extremely well; they have connected their lives together with an oath. Their servants travel with them, heavily armed. Everyone is on horseback and has been trained, alert for danger and protected with all kinds of armour.

The friends even have plenty of money for a change. When you're going on an adventure, it is important to make the crossing in the right ship.

The vessel of Jesus is both a sailing ship and a fishing boat. It is a wondrous mix of working and resting, playing with the wind and hard labour. This ship is not too big and not too small. It is a ship that requires collaboration. It is the ship of all for one and one for all. This is the ship that sails on a mission that is bigger than the sum of the lives of all its crew. And the most important thing is that Jesus has taken His place at the helm, at the stern.

The storms in your life are no regular storms

Accompanied by countless other vessels, Jesus' ship sails into the night. Quickly, a storm emerges. And not just any storm. Mark and Luke both describe the storm using the ominous word *lailaps* ("hurricane" in today's terminology). There were storms, and then there was a *lailaps*. A tough fisherman wouldn't shy away from a little storm, but a *lailaps*... that was something else. In a *lailaps*, cold air comes crashing off the mountain slopes, only to fatally collide with the warm air above the lake. Deadly whirlwinds are the result. The air around the ship of Jesus turns into a furious swirling chaos. And not just that. Matthew describes the same storm using the word *seismos*, which means quake – a seaquake. That night, Jesus' ship isn't just facing countless whirlwinds, but also enormous tsunami-like waves. *Lailaps* and *seismos*: the storm of the century. All forces of nature join hands to get to the ship of Jesus and His friends. Jesus must die.

From the very beginning, the forces of evil have got it in for Jesus. Herod orders all baby boys in Bethlehem to be killed, hoping that Jesus is among them. The scholars try to kill Jesus six times; the devil tries to conquer Him through seduction; demons challenge His power; and now here, we see nature being utilized as a tool for darkness to disable Jesus. That is the essence of this stormy night at the lake: an accumulation of the powers of evil to destroy Jesus. The storms that will be used against us during our quest will have the same nature. The storms in your life are not regular storms. They are battles for life and death. They are the powers of hell doing everything they can to squeeze God's life out of you.

Fleeing in yourself

This night describes human life in a nutshell: the initiative of Jesus, the crossing over the big lake, the nightfall, the raging storm, the survival. And Jesus? He sleeps. For a while now. Peacefully at the stern. To the other side, while sleeping...

That's part of a quest, too. You'll be on your own. It may even seem as if God has abandoned you, just when you needed Him most. Now that the pressure on your life is increasing, your marriage isn't going smoothly, you like your job less and less, your children are slipping away, illness is destroying you, and evil seems to triumph – that is the moment that Jesus is sleeping on the stern.

It would have hardly made any difference if He had been dead. That's how sound asleep He is.

The disciples do everything they can to keep the ship afloat. They fight for their lives. In blind survival mode, they bail water from the boat, they call each other names, and they say their prayers. In times of storm, we often swing our fists wildly around us, wounding the people who are closest to us.

At a certain point, the battle becomes so fierce that some people close their eyes to everything that is happening. They withdraw into themselves. They flee.

A German Christian, who lived in Nazi Germany during World War II, explained that his family's church was located at a railway station. During a Sunday service, they heard a steam whistle in the distance. The believers heard a locomotive approach them and after that the rattling of an endless line of cattle cars. The cars held people, screaming, crying, begging, hysterical – Jews on their way to the gas chambers. The first time that train passed, the members of the church remained seated in shock. On the next Sunday, they heard the steam whistle again during the service. But this time, they didn't sit still. They got up and started to sing. As the train approached, they would sing louder... simply so they wouldn't have to hear the screaming of the doomed. It became a ritual: every Sunday, the steam whistle; every Sunday, the singing.

After the war, the man described his experiences, and he said:

> *Every night, in my sleep, I hear that steam whistle. I hear that train approaching... God forgive me, God forgive all those people who call themselves Christians, but did nothing...*

God forgive all those people who flee into themselves, who – with Jesus in their boat – close their eyes to the storm, to the darkness, and who sing too loudly, work too hard, run away too fast, drink too much, watch too much TV.

God forgive all those boys who keep dragging their hessian sack.

How did you hold up in your ship during the storm? Did

you break a lot of things? Did you wound people, the people closest to you, as you were swinging your fists in terror? Did you carry the urge to flee with your hessian sack? Did you start singing too loudly, working too hard, surfing the Internet too often?

The ultimate question

Suddenly, a couple of disciples come to their senses. While, in their fear, they were only thinking about themselves, a few of them suddenly realize: "But what about Jesus? Shouldn't He be doing anything? He can at least help us to bail water. It is really not acceptable to drown while sleeping. If anything, die fighting, like a real man."

Through the storm, they stumble towards Jesus, wake him up roughly, and, trying to drown out the noise of the storm, they shout: "Teacher, do You not care that we are perishing?"

Isn't that the ultimate question?

It is the question of the concentration camps, the question from Haiti, the question from Rwanda, the question from North Korea. Our question: "Do you not care that we are perishing? Do you not care that your entire venture is failing?"

Why Jesus intervened

Jesus wakes up, rubs His eyes, assesses the situation, and gets to His feet. All paintings and drawings of the events of this night show that Jesus is no longer standing on the stern, but instead is holding on to the mast, putting his foot forward. He takes charge. Jesus rises, amid the raging storm! It is the same word used by the disciples when they engage each other on Easter Sunday: "He is risen! He is risen indeed!" Jesus has risen from His sleep, from His unconsciousness, from His death. See Him standing there, His hand on the mast, foot forward, watching the storm with a divine twinkle in His eyes. And there, amid all the darkness that wants to overwhelm Him, He speaks that word, that one word, upward to the *lailaps* – "Silence!" – and that one word downward to the wild, raging waves of the *seismos* – "Quiet!" "Be gagged," it literally says. Jesus gags the gaping maw of the water, hungry for 13 male bodies.

Jesus was asleep, but was His sleep a sign of weakness? No! It was a sign of His strength. Jesus was so in control that He was even able to sleep quietly in the midst of a raging storm. He was certain that He would not drown that night, since it was not yet His time.

Jesus does not panic over our storms. He does not lose balance over our discomfort. He never has to fight or flee, since He is the ruler of heaven and earth, the expeller of demons, the healer of illness, the changer of people, and the silencer of storms.

Why did Jesus intervene? To prevent the storm from winning? No. He intervened because the disciples needed Him to. He didn't intervene to regain control; He intervened to show that He has the power.

Perhaps that is exactly what you need right now. There is a part of you that wants to join Jesus on His adventure, but the storms of life overwhelm you. And Jesus? As far as you can tell, He has been sleeping for ages on the aft deck. Buried. His role in your life is over. That means that now is the time to wake Jesus up. It doesn't really matter how or what you say to Him. Even if you pose Him the ultimate question: "Don't You care that my life is in ruins?" Maybe

Jesus has been waiting for this moment. Maybe He wants to be awakened by you. This is the moment that He has longed for. He wants to rise in your ship and take control. He wants to take you along on His mythical quest to expand His kingdom.

And then, after things have settled down, He would like to discuss something with you. Why were you so afraid? Why did you lack faith? Why did you resort to fighting and fleeing? These questions are not reproachful, not pitying or judgmental. They are sincere questions, loving, penetrating, intended to help you discover what else you're carrying around in your hessian sack.

Only my skin is afraid

Max Meyers, a pilot at the Mission Aviation Fellowship (MAF), tells about one of his flights with four Papuan warriors as passengers. None of the warriors had ever flown before, and of course this was the flight during which Max ran into a heavy storm. When he looked over his shoulder, he saw that three of the four Papuans were holding on to one another, scared to death. Their dark faces were green with misery and drenched in sweat. However, his fourth passenger was completely calm.

> *"Aren't you afraid?," I asked him. "Only my skin is afraid," the Papuan replied... "I see the mountains. They are so close. I can see the trees and the rocks as they rush by. I see the rain and hear the drops tapping against the window. I see clouds everywhere around me. Everything I see around me frightens me. I didn't know your big bird would shake that heavily when you flew it.*

There is a lot to be afraid of, but my fear is only as deep as my skin. You know, I know the one who has made the mountains. I know the one who has made the rocks and the trees. I know the one who has made the clouds and rain for us today. He has told me that I don't have to be afraid. Why? Because He lives inside of me. Inside my skin. And He has promised me that He would never abandon me. And that is why I am not afraid."

Do you have Jesus under your skin?

With Jesus under your skin, you can respond differently during the storms of life. Do you see Jesus sleep? Just go and lie down next to him. Let the storms rage, let hell shriek, let the wind howl. When Jesus is at peace, then so am I.

It is the ultimate lesson of this night, the lesson you'll only learn during the quest: Are you willing to place your faith in a sleeping Jesus?

Are you willing to leave the safe harbour behind, to live through the storm and allow your male heart to be formed?

Are you willing to go on an adventure, even with a sleeping Jesus?

Rather alive than dead

If so, don't forget: a sleeping Jesus isn't dead. Even a Jesus in the grave of Joseph of Arimathea does what He wants. Even a dead Jesus rules.

During the period that we refer to him as "dead", Jesus crushed the head of the snake, ransacked the realm of the dead, broke the power of sin over our lives, and achieved the biggest victory in the history of man.

In His death, Jesus has achieved more than all the world leaders combined during their lifetimes. From His grave, Jesus has achieved greater victories than all the Roman emperors were able to accomplish from their thrones. I believe that Jesus' death really ticked off the devil. If only he had allowed Jesus to live. Because, while Jesus annoyed Satan to death during His lifetime, in death He ransacked Satan's entire graveyard and made him the laughing stock of all heavenly realms. In the devil's opinion, it's better to have a living Jesus than a dead one. Alive, He was bad enough. Dead, He was a disaster.

Who is He?

That is the question that concludes this evening tour. Goosebumps. Healing the sick? OK. Chasing away demons? That's fine. But controlling the forces of nature? That's a whole different ballgame. Until now, the disciples had stuck to the principle that says: "Jesus really has a lot of abilities. He has so much power." But this night, they will take it to the next level. They travel from "what" to "who". Past the actions, they reach His person – a person you don't want to fight with, a person that it is better to obey and follow... towards Gadara, the area occupied by darkness.

When the storms hit your life, allow the power of the Spirit to calm you. Do not tell God how big and dangerous the storm is, but tell the storm how overwhelming and awesome your God is.

Even when He's asleep.

7

Hunting like Nimrod

*That same evening, M. de Tréville announced
this good news [that d'Artagnan would be
promoted to Musketeer] to the three Musketeers
and d'Artagnan, inviting all four to breakfast
with him next morning. D'Artagnan was beside
himself with joy. We know that the dream of his
life had been to become a Musketeer. The three
friends were likewise greatly delighted.*

ALEXANDRE DUMAS

The choice to put your faith in a sleeping Jesus is like taking the first step on an adventurous path towards a beautiful destination. If we are willing to accept this adventure with Jesus, He will lead us to the point from which our lives will be dominated by four characteristics: servitude, giving, taking responsibility, and the willingness to sacrifice. As Jesus took His disciples under His wing for nearly three years, He will take us under His wing as well. He will bring us closer and closer to our final destination: life as a servant of the King.

What it is truly about

In this respect, it is important to distinguish different phases of following Jesus. It all started with a life-altering encounter with Jesus. The lives of the disciples were overturned. In the vicinity of Jesus, they found the rest, inspiration, and sense of meaning that they had longed for. Still, their commitment to follow Jesus was not firm. We even see the disciples leave Jesus for a couple of weeks at the beginning to return to fishing. However, Jesus doesn't give up, and He decides to pay His friends a visit. This time, He challenges them to take a radical step: "Come, follow me," He repeatedly says. Peter, Andrew, James, John, and the others leave their work, families, homes, and home town behind and decide to follow Jesus full-time. Jesus turns the follower into a loner. He requires radical choices. In this phase, we don't see the disciples say or do anything. They only follow, watch, and listen. For nine months, they take in the basic principles of the kingdom of God. Then, another moment of opportunity presents itself: the formal calling of the Twelve. In the months thereafter, Jesus directs His followers more and more to the foreground. He sends them on mission trips, asks them to care for people, and gives them the power to heal and the authority to preach. Through trial and error, but still under the direct supervision of Jesus, the disciples learn what it means to live with God.

Eventually, the disciples find themselves at the weekend that the world changes: the weekend of the crucifixion and resurrection. Everything changes. Jesus only appears occasionally, and after 40 days He goes to heaven. Ten days later, the Holy Spirit is poured out. He takes over the supervisory duties from Jesus. And successfully so. A megachurch is formed in Jerusalem, and in spite of cruel persecution, the gospel is distributed across the world.

In my (Henk's) book *De Leerling* ("The Student"), I work out this process in greater detail. But the point we'd like to make here is as follows: *living with Jesus is a process.* Your conversion is not God's final goal. Eliminating sin is not God's final goal. Serving, helping others, or evangelizing from place to place is not God's final goal. God's plan for your life is to lead or train you to become a musketeer, an elite soldier of the King, living a life based on servitude, giving, responsibility, and the willingness to sacrifice.

Goldfish, couch potatoes, and might-have-beens

Some Christians never grow beyond their conversion phase. They keep bouncing back and forth in terms of spirituality: a little towards Jesus, a little away from Jesus, a little towards Jesus, and a little away again. They don't have the radicalism in their lives. They live like a goldfish that can't escape from its bowl. Every time the hand of the Owner grabs him from the bowl to throw him into the ocean, he jumps right back into the bowl, because he's too comfortable swimming in circles.

Other Christians remain stuck in the first phase of radicalism: they follow Jesus and are watching and listening, but they do nothing; they are couch potatoes. American churches are packed with people who have heard thousands of sermons, but haven't even put ten of them into practice. Their heads are getting bigger and fuller all the time, but their faith muscles are shrivelling. It is dangerous to grow a big head. Sin and blame remain as major themes in these Christians. They have sharp minds and can easily tell you where a certain doctrine goes wrong. But how to live life? They don't have a clue.

Others are willing to do things, but not too much and not forever. They live as might-have-beens. Everyone sees that they have something special in them, but one way or the other, it never comes out. They are like an eel in a bucket of slime. You simply can't catch them. You can't restrict them. This is the case with many young people. On the one hand, the world is at your feet. Everything is possible. On the other hand, you have a wife and children at home who also require your attention. Your plate is more than full. How would you fit in serving the church? How can you take on additional responsibility for the kingdom of God?

What would history have looked like if Peter, John, and all those other followers of Jesus hadn't been willing to take on their responsibility?

Do musketeers still exist?

God is looking for men who are willing to go all out for Him, who want to become musketeers. J. Oswald Sanders says:

> *The Bible shows us that when God finds someone willing to lead, to commit to discipleship, and to take responsibility for other people, this person will be used to the end.*

Serving – instead of wanting to be served or to be seen. Giving – instead of receiving or collecting. Taking responsibility – instead of running away from it. Being willing to sacrifice – instead of self-protection and false security. But can God find enough musketeers? Are there still people who think that it is an honour to give their life in service to the King? The Bible shows us a heartbreaking cry of God on a couple of occasions. In Isaiah 6, Isaiah is allowed to take a look at heaven. He sees impressively tall angels, and he experiences the crushing power of God. And then there's the question: "Whom shall I send? And who will go for us?" (Isaiah 6:8)

Who will go for Us? The Trinity is looking for help. And in Ezekiel 22:

> *I looked for someone among them who would build up the wall and stand before me in the gap on behalf of the land so I would not have to destroy it, but I found no one. So I will pour out my wrath on them and consume them with my fiery anger (Ezekiel 22:30–31)*

Did God want to destroy the city? No. He wanted to protect and build it up, but there was nobody – not one person – who considered it an honour to be God's servant. And again, in Isaiah:

> *He saw that there was no one, he was appalled that there was no one to intervene; so his own arm achieved salvation for him, and his own righteousness sustained him. (Isaiah 59:16)*

Imagine having helped ten friends move over the past ten years. They were intense but wonderful Saturdays. It cost you time and effort, but they were your friends, so you did it with love. Now you're moving, and you need help. You call your ten friends. Nobody can help.

Nobody!

That, multiplied by billions (people) and applied, not to moving, but to the level of life and death... it gives you an indication of what God must feel. After all that He did for us. After Jesus' suffering and crucifixion. After the cross.

And you wonder: Does all of humanity consist of goldfish, couch potatoes, and might-have-beens? Do musketeers still exist?

Do you have the heart? That is the first question. Do you have the heart to serve, to give, to take responsibility, and to sacrifice yourself? For the King?

Ask that question later, in heaven

Stan Dale, a former commando, had heard the voice of God and wanted to reach the unsaved tribes of Papua New Guinea with the gospel. Although he was married, he travelled into the wilds with his wife to tell a few cannibals about God's love. Stan paved the way. After he had made a landing strip for the plane with his bare hands, his wife joined him. They had five children together. As a family, they lived among hostile tribes, for whom child sacrifices were completely normal. Two of their most loyal Papuan converts were murdered by hostile tribes. When Stan tried to rescue a couple of friends during an ambush, he was hit by five spears. Severely injured, he climbed over the high ridges until he reached his house. After his recovery, he kept working tirelessly to bring the people to Jesus. During an exploration, a hostile tribe attacked Stan and his companion. After a wild chase, the warriors were able to capture Stan. They killed him with over 50 spears. And then, they ate him.

Father of five children, husband to a sweet, brave woman. Was Stan's lifestyle a responsible one? Ask that question later, in heaven, of all the Papuans who found God's mercy through the pioneering evangelism of Stan and his family.

Stan had heard the voice. He was willing to pay the

price. He died on a mission, and as always, the blood of this martyr proved to be the seed of a growing church.

Do you have the heart?

The heart of Father Kuric

A couple of months ago, I paid a visit to a beautiful campus in Africa. It was spaciously designed, with beautiful trees and plants. It was a Thursday afternoon, and the university teams were playing a soccer match on the freshly mown field. It was a place of great beauty.

And tragedy.

Because this was the Ecole Technique Officiele (ETO) in Kigali, Rwanda. During the outbreak of the genocide in early April 1994, about 2,500 terrified Tutsis sought shelter on this campus, along with 90 Belgian paratroopers who were stationed there. The school was surrounded. Thousands of Hutus with war paint, whistles, machetes, iron bats, and all other kinds of primitive weaponry, increased the pressure on the UN soldiers. On 11 April, after the first refugees had arrived, the UN soldiers were ordered to withdraw from the school campus.

They packed their weapons.

They got in their trucks.

And they drove away.

With the last UN truck still in sight, the murderous Hutus rushed onto the campus to kill every single person there.

The movie *Shooting Dogs* tells the story of the horrific massacre at the ETO. In the movie, Father Christopher plays an important role. He is the only white man who refuses to flee with the UN soldiers, and he stays loyal to the local population. While saving a number of children, he is murdered.

Father Christopher didn't really exist. But his role was inspired by the actions of Vjekoslav Kuric. This Croatian priest was one of the few white people in Rwanda who refused to leave during the genocide, and, according to witnesses, he saved thousands of lives. "I chose to come to Rwanda and to build the kingdom of God. I want to share in their joy, suffering, and risks." During and after the genocide, Kuric was threatened with death countless times, but he continued to give of himself for the people of Rwanda. He even built a hospital. On 30 January 1998, he was shot to death in Kigali.

The UN soldiers and Father Kuric tell a story about the heart. The UN soldiers were prepared to serve. They were in Rwanda and did what they could, until danger came too close. When their servitude endangered their own lives, they decided to listen to the ingrained tendency, dormant and hidden in that hessian sack on their backs, to run from responsibility; and they left. With drastic consequences. Father Kuric remained loyal to his heart until the bitter – glorious – end.

What story does your heart tell?

Perhaps God won't send you to the Papuans or to Rwanda, but don't worry, there are plenty of other people who need your help. A question shared by many men is: *What purpose does God have for my life?* A couple of weeks ago, I asked a dozen men to think about this question for six weeks, and the men happily accepted my invitation. "What is it that I live for? What are my goals here on earth?" A way to clarify this question is by looking at what turns your heart cold. And warm. What touches you?

In Colossians 1:24 Paul writes the enigmatic words:

> *Now I rejoice in what I am suffering for you, and*
> *I fill up in my flesh what is still lacking in regard*
> *to Christ's afflictions, for the sake of his body,*
> *which is the church.*

Is something lacking in the suffering of Jesus? Apparently. Jesus did what He had to do, and at the same time, extra life energy and willingness to sacrifice oneself is required to apply the lessons of Jesus' life in all kinds of situations. Jesus died 2,000 years ago for all Rwandans, but He needed a Father Kuric to make His love visible – through suffering – during the nightmare of the genocide. Jesus had long ago paid the price for the cannibals in the jungles of Papua New Guinea, but He needed a Stan Dale, who was willing actually to bring Jesus to them – through suffering. To make the church as it should be, men and women are needed who are willing to suffer and, in doing so, to continue Jesus' work and to realize it in places where the church has insufficient visibility.

What rock can God place on your heart?

During the 4th Musketeer weekend in Scotland in 2010, a mountain was the central theme on the second day: The Devil's Point. The path to this menacing black solid rock went through a valley, with high ridges on both sides and overwhelming natural beauty. After about six hours, the teams reached The Devil's Point. At the base of the mountain, there is a bothy, a mountain cabin in which hikers can spend the night for free. Each team was given a brief moment of contemplation, in which they were asked which heart they wished to take into the world: the heart of the UN soldiers or the heart of Father Kuric? After the period of contemplation, every man looked for a rock. This rock symbolized the burden God was allowed to give them. What rock can God place on your heart? In what field would you like to join Jesus in His suffering, for His kingdom? The men each looked for their rock and were then allowed to enter the bothy, one by one. In the bothy, they found a burning torch. By the light of the torch, large photos of social injustice were visible – poverty, violence, child labour, illness. Which rock can God place on your heart? Most men came out crying. Subsequently, they were asked to climb The Devil's Point while carrying the heavy rock in their arms. What bastion of the devil would you like to level? Which mountain of evil do you want to climb? Where do you want to see God's glory and love break through? The men climbed. And prayed. And climbed. And prayed.

About halfway up, they had to stop. From that point up to the peak, there was nothing but snow and ice. Irresponsible. Impossible. The men were told: "You made it all the way here. Great job. Jesus climbed the entire mountain. He reached the places that we can't reach. He has conquered evil."

Men found their mission. For one man, the rock symbolized the foster child he would meet for the very first time the next week. He decided to carry the rock throughout the trip to the base camp, in his backpack. "After a while, I no longer felt the weight of the rock." Two months after that weekend, he was talking about meeting his foster daughter and how he had been dreading it. "But," he said, "that was two months ago, and now this girl is in my backpack forever. I don't even feel the weight any more. The rock is now a feather." Another man talked about how the process of caring for his son, suffering from autism, was a struggle, every single day. "That is the rock God has given me, and I want to carry it as well as I can. I want to serve my son and guide him through this life."

Where does your heart lie, and are you willing to pay for it?

A Musketeer told me how his life had always been about comfort. Everything had to be effortless. His life had to be comfortable, without worries, without stress, without problems. He did whatever he liked and avoided the things that he considered too big a challenge. Now, at the mountain, he had to find his passion. What was he against? What was he in favour of? He chose a beautiful, big rock. So large that everyone could see it. He was big and strong, and he was going to carry this large rock. He started his journey to the top, and it was heavier than he had anticipated. Halfway through, he was all alone. Nobody around.

> And that was my moment. I was carrying around
> that heavy rock, and I figured that I might as
> well swap it for a light rock. That was easier.
> And nobody would see me switching my rock.
> As I was standing at this proverbial crossroad, it
> suddenly struck me like lightning. This was the
> story of my life. I had always been looking for the
> easy way out. Nothing was allowed to require any
> effort on my part. I would get a lighter rock. But
> not any more. I decided to keep my rock, and I
> struggled my way up there.

Before that, he had never wanted to take on too many responsibilities in his church. After his Devil's Point experience, that changed. If there was a challenge, he would accept it. Several weeks later, two elders visited him. Reluctantly, they asked whether he would consider accepting the office of elder. "I was expecting you," he replied. "I am happy to accept this task." Then, he told the baffled elders what had made him decide to take this step.

Hunting like Nimrod

When God places a rock on your heart, it is important how you interpret it. Not everyone has to preach. Not everyone has to become a missionary. Being a Musketeer means that you are willing to develop and use the skills, talents, and creativity that God has given you to an optimal extent. In Genesis 10:8–9, we see how God enjoys someone who is good at what he does:

> Cush was the father of Nimrod, who became a
> mighty warrior on the earth. He was a mighty
> hunter before the Lord; that is why it is said,
> "Like Nimrod, a mighty hunter before the Lord."

Was Nimrod a priest? Was he a writer of devotional books? Was he a pastoral worker?

Nimrod was a hunter.

He searched, chased, waited, aimed, shot, killed, skinned. He was a hunter. And not just any hunter. He was the best hunter in the world at that time. He hunted in the manner that God wanted people to hunt. He hunted in such a formidable way that he drew God's attention. God watched from the heavens, watching Nimrod work, and He thought to Himself: "Such a great shot! So much power, so much courage! Wonderful! What a hunter, that Nimrod." Nimrod's hunting skills became proverbial: "Like Nimrod a mighty hunter before the Lord."

What is your thing? Leadership? Management? Teaching? Interactions with children? Construction? Transportation? Making music? It doesn't matter what you do, as long as you make sure that you're the best you can be at it. According to Malcolm Gladwell, who conducted a study into the factors that enable people to excel, it requires about 10,000 hours of practice to achieve excellence. Or in other words, three hours a day for ten years.

Make sure you'll be proverbial in your skill. Learn to "hunt like Nimrod".

Don't wait. The best day to enter this new phase of following Jesus is today. Time after time, the Bible encourages us to act. Don't postpone; don't delegate. You've been a goldfish, couch potato, or might-have-been long enough. Remove the habit of avoiding responsibility from your hessian sack. You're allowed to act. Today.

When you focus your skill on the rock placed on your heart by God, brace yourself. New books will have to be written. About you. Living as a Musketeer.

Just do it.

8

Three musketeers

> *"Ah, ah! but what's going on in the city yonder?"*
> *said Athos.*
>   *"They are beating the general alarm."*
>   *The four friends listened, and the sound of the*
> *drum plainly reached them.*
>   *"You see, they are going to send a whole*
> *regiment against us," said Athos.*
>   *"You don't think of holding out against a whole*
> *regiment, do you?" Porthos asked.*
>   *"Why not?" the Musketeer said.*
>
> ALEXANDRE DUMAS

For centuries, God has been calling on men to "hunt like Nimrod"; to live as musketeers. One of these men was Gideon.

Visit from heaven

God's assignment for Gideon comes at a time in which a coalition of cruel desert people has been tormenting Israel for seven straight years. In a devastating wave of cruelty, they rob men of their honour, women of their beauty, children of their future, the country of its income, and the cattle of their lives. As soon as the enemy has disappeared over the horizon, the survivors dejectedly crawl from their caverns and holes. The irony is that they have asked for it. They had placed their bets on Baal, the God of storm, rain, and crop growth. But Baal hadn't kept his end of the deal. They had also bet on Asherah, the mother-goddess of love, war, and fertility. But she hadn't kept her end of the bargain either. Or at least not entirely, because there was in fact a war, regardless of all temple prostitution and child sacrifices. And now, they are plucked alive, humiliated to the bone, extremely poor, and naked. Their final scream of despair reaches heaven. And God is God. He doesn't close the book, but starts a new chapter. The Angel of the Lord sits down under a tree and tells Gideon:

> *"The Lord is with you, mighty warrior... Go in the strength you have and save Israel out of Midian's hand. Am I not sending you?" (Judges 6:12, 14)*

When Gideon asks what would give him the power to do so, God replies: "I will be with you." (Judges 6:16)

Spot on. Gideon's life will never be the same again.

Don't postpone; begin

The invitation to "hunt like Nimrod", to live as a musketeer, to act like a hero, is there. For each of us. Which rock did God place on your heart? What mission will you focus on?

One thing is essential when it comes to completing a mission: *beginning*.

It all starts with taking action.

If we consider the life of Gideon, beginning seems to be the hardest part of his entire adventure with God. Although the Angel gives him the qualification "brave warrior", it still feels like that title is incorrect. "Brave" doesn't call to mind a man who threshes wheat in a wine press, fearful of being seen by the enemy. "Brave" doesn't depict someone asking questions and making objections in response to a request to go to battle. Nor does it call to mind the image of an insecure man, looking for confirmation and requesting signs several times. Still, that is exactly what Gideon does. He completes his first assignment (destroying the Baal altar, the Asherah pole, and sacrificing the beautiful bull of his father on an altar for God with the help of ten men, in the middle of the night, out of fear for his family and fellow citizens). When God asks him to fight Midian's army, he spreads a sheepskin twice to make absolutely sure that he is doing what God asked. That is not a sign of faith; it's more like the opposite. Later on in the adventure, God gives him another encouragement, through a frightening dream of his adversaries in the enemy camp. Gideon seizes the opportunity with both hands to find confirmation for what God had already promised: You will be victorious.

Then, why is Gideon a brave hero? Why does he find a place in the renowned gallery of heroes of faith in Hebrews 11? What does God see in him?

His heart.

God knows that Gideon will take on his mission, despite his fears. That is what makes Gideon a hero.

Why do so many men want to live their mission, but fail to do so?

Fear.

"Frightened" is at the top of the list of things that men don't want to be. That is why a man's biggest fear is to be seen as afraid. And that is why we lock ourselves up. We crawl away behind thick walls. On the inside, a man can tremble like a leaf, while, on the outside, he displays great strength. Driven by the desire to be considered a real man, he is able to hide behind a mask of decisiveness and control. But the tragic thing is that, because of that mask of false bravery, not only does he have to live with his fear, but also with the fear that someone will find out. Sooner or later, that gets to you.

"You make me feel very itchy"

In the week before an XCC of The 4th Musketeer, the phone rang. It was Jos, an estate agent at our church. "Listen. I am having serious doubts about going this weekend. I am in total panic right now. I feel stuck in my work and family, I am incredibly insecure, and I simply can't think straight, let alone make decisions. But above all, I am scared. I am unable to comprehend that whole XCC. I even contacted my general practitioner and a psychologist, and they both said: 'We strongly advise you not to go!'"

Based on everything he told me after that, I knew where he was coming from. Regardless, I tried my best to keep him on board, and said, "I am deeply convinced that you should go."

I truly meant it. We talked. Jos admitted that he was afraid of being exposed, afraid that he would no longer be able to pretend that everything was going great. He was afraid that the truth about what was going on inside of him would come out, that he would have to admit that, in fact, he was terrified. And he didn't want to do that.

Eventually, Jos decided to go, and with that decision, he took the most important step in overcoming his fear. With his team, Jos didn't just honestly express his fears, but also his emotions; for instance, towards team member Jan. Jan is the mission pastor at our church, a full-time position. He frequently preaches in worship services. During the XCC, Jan tried to connect with Jos, to encourage him... to the annoyance of Jos, who did everything he could to avoid and ignore Jan. Near the climax of the weekend, when all men knelt before the cross in exhaustion, something miraculous happened. Jan walked towards Jos and said, "I love you, brother." Jos was somewhat perplexed, but he decided to be completely honest and said, "Then, I have to share something with you, Jan. You make me feel very itchy every time I see you. I am constantly annoyed by you, in a very unpleasant way. Every time you preach at church, I am annoyed that I didn't know in advance, so that I could have stayed home." Jan was shocked, and said that he never knew. Then, the tears began to flow, and the men embraced without any words. It covered everything – forgiveness, liberation. Jan and Jos now have a very special connection. Jan says, "Every time I see Jos, I tell him that I am proud of him, because he was courageous enough to express his feelings."

The XCC proved to be a turning point for Jos. Prior to that weekend, panic and anguish controlled his life. After the weekend, there was peace of God and strength to calmly get back on his feet. The weekend changed his life. The main characteristic of brave heroes is that they overcome fear by honestly expressing it.

What is stopping you from entering a new phase of following Jesus? What makes you postpone or delegate? What are you afraid of?

Afraid that others might discover who you really are? Afraid to be a father, because you didn't have a great father? Afraid to do your job, because you don't have an honest boss and you have colleagues who work much more efficiently than you can? Afraid to be a husband, because you don't know anything about feelings, perhaps?

Adrift by the Spirit

Gideon started his mission to live in spite of his fear. The moment that Gideon actually begins his life is the moment when he blows the trumpet and mobilizes an army. It is no coincidence that this happens immediately after the sentence: "Then the spirit of the Lord came upon Gideon." (Judges 6:34)

What a sentence! God's Spirit falls on Gideon and grabs him by the throat. However, the literal translation of the text is even more powerful: "The spirit of the Lord wore Gideon." God's Spirit wears Gideon like a suit of armour. The Spirit possesses Gideon's entire being. Everyone who faces Gideon now faces the Spirit in him. Gideon is packed with Spirit. Poor Midianites. "Then, the Spirit of the Lord wore Gideon." Without this sentence, Gideon would have remained stuck in the backyard of his father. Without the Spirit of the Lord, there is no enthusiasm and actual passion. We'll keep living "sensibly", and we'll never truly begin living the mission that God has planned for us. Or, as Kierkegaard says:

> Our time is substantially wise, maybe – on
> average – it knows more than any generation
> before it, but it has no passion. Everybody knows
> a lot, we all know what path to take, and we

all know what paths we could take, but nobody
actually dares to walk it.

Are there areas of fear in your life? Be careful! Of the
32,000 troops in the army of Gideon, 22,000 men go
home, because they're afraid. They are not happy with their
lives, but they don't have the courage to do anything about
it. The Spirit wants to send these men into the world. Fear
pushes men back into their chairs. In what areas of your life
do you need God's Spirit of love, strength, and prudence to
eliminate every form of cowardice? Discuss it honestly with
other brothers, and be wary of the consequences...

Source of inspiration...

Gideon begins, enters into battle, and gives it everything
he's got. And he needs to. A situation that pitted 300 men
against 135,000 enemy soldiers required commitment and
intelligent thinking. He proves to be a brilliant strategist,
who is able to utilize the power of illusion and the element
of surprise to the maximum extent. Being allowed to share
in the work of God brings out the best in a man. God uses
the chaos caused by Gideon, and He lets the desert people
fight each other:

> *Israelites from Naphtali, Asher and all Manasseh*
> *were called out, and they pursued the Midianites.*
> *Gideon sent messengers throughout the hill*
> *country of Ephraim, saying, "Come down against*
> *the Midianites and seize the waters of the*
> *Jordan..." So all the men of Ephraim were called*
> *out and they seized the waters of the Jordan as*
> *far as Beth Barah. They also captured two of*

> *the Midianite leaders, Oreb and Zeeb… They*
> *pursued the Midianites. (Judges 7:23–25)*

Men inspire others when they overcome their fear and use their gifts in service of the Lord as brave heroes. The men who had gone home eventually rejoin the others in battle. An older, wise leader said: "We have a significant lack of divinely inspired men. I see way too few of them." Men are supposed to be sources of inspiration for other men. Are you a source of inspiration for others?

Don't fall back: persevere

In living your mission, persevering is as important as beginning. Persevering means that you stay loyal to your home, that you fight to preserve what you have there, that, after a hesitant start, you don't get so consumed by your mission in the world that you compromise the dynamics of peace in your own home. There are countless children of pastors who have turned their backs on the church, because dad had all the attention, love, and time in the world for lost souls, but not for his own children. The same applies to men who lose themselves in any other form of career. Only then, the children feel differently towards their absence. A young man told me (Theo) that he was aware of a gaping father wound caused by an almost complete absence of his father. Every minute that he wasn't working for his boss, his father was working for the church. His son tried to talk to him about it, but he couldn't get the message across.

"It is what it is."

Shammah, the lion

Someone who embodied the spirit of fighting for your home was Shammah, son of Agee. Shammah was one of the three most prominent heroes of David. One day, the Philistines had gathered their troops at Lehi, presumably a city in the tribe of Judah, near the border with the Philistines. There was a small field with lentils there. Until then, the Philistines had been superior to the Israelites. But that changed in David's time, partly because of men like Shammah. As the army of Israel fled, Shammah stationed himself at the small piece of (seemingly insignificant) land. He fought like a lion, and no Philistine was able to drive him out. The Lord honoured Shammah's efforts and gave Israel a major victory. Shammah was able to assess the true value of that little field and fought for the piece of land in the tribal territory of Judah. He fought for home.

Men often dream of big, visible successes at work or at church. But it is essential that persevering outdoors blends with persevering at home, in the small and invisible. Oswald Chambers says:

> *One can successfully overcome a crisis, but that's*
> *not the same as constantly struggling, day by day,*
> *to the Glory of God, with nobody witnessing,*
> *if one cannot enter the limelight and no one is*
> *paying any attention to us.*

For some people, beginning at home means turning off the television and celebrating intimacy. For others, it means breaking the silence and starting a conversation, or to stop ignoring and paying someone a visit, or to stop judging and start encouraging. Not just being an example of resilience and vitality for your colleagues, but for your children as well. It sometimes requires a radical change.

"You must lead"

During one of the XCCs, Erwin, one of the participants, was strongly told by God that he had to "begin at home". After an exhausting trip on the second day, he arrived at base camp. He still had a 45-minute trip through a cave left to do that day. Erwin was determined to enter the cave, but just as determined that he didn't want to lead. Into the cave — fine. Lead? Absolutely not! Things didn't work out that way. Regardless of his intentions, Erwin led the way. Trying to get a grip with his hands and feet on slippery walls and hanging from ledges, Erwin struggled through narrow gaps. Things went well, until he found out that they were going in circles. The men, with Erwin in the lead, had to go back. Erwin:

> Sweating and dabbling, I finally reached the starting point. Gasping for air, I emerged from the cave. I was exhausted, angry, and indignant. What was the point?
> It wasn't until the next night that God told me: "Erwin, be a priest in your family. You must lead the way."

Another Musketeer says about the weekend:

> A lot has changed. I have started praying a lot more with my wife. We give priority to "us" time and moments together with God. It feels so great. Where we used to spend our nights eating chips and watching television, we now truly take

*the time to work on our relationship with God.
Consciously leaving the TV off, and finding better
ways to spend your leisure time... Sometimes you
think you're tired and you want to give yourself
permission to spend an evening in front of the
television. But then, I try to make conscious
choices and do chores in and around the house.
I used to constantly postpone that, but now I try
to do these things as quickly as possible. And
my wife loves it. I have also become a different
father. I try to consciously give everyone time and
attention. I try to give them more.*

Implementing rituals

Shammah fought for the small field and won. It may help
to mark the transition from serving outdoors to persevering
at home with a ritual – a cup of coffee at the gas station on
your way home; briefly parking your car on the side of the
road and praying for your family; finishing your phone calls
before you get into the house. Give yourself time to switch.
Go for your field. Without victories at home, you have no
foundation for victories outdoors.

Once we are able to serve at home, we have no reason not
to face the danger as soon as we can. We require Jonathan's
mentality if we really want to complete the mission God has
placed in our hearts.

Not the path of the least, but the most, resistance

Jonathan, the son of Saul and friend of David, was done
with it. The Israelites were at war with the Philistines, but

it wasn't an equal battle. Back then, there was no sword or spear to be found in Israel, because of the Philistines. Only Saul and Jonathan had a decent weapon.

One day, Jonathan decided to go to a Philistine garrison to seek out the battle, his reason being: "Perhaps the Lord will act in our behalf. Nothing can hinder the Lord from saving, whether by many or by few." (1 Samuel 14:6b)

His armour bearer thought it was an excellent plan: "Go ahead; I am with you heart and soul." (1 Samuel 14:7)

Then, Jonathan revealed his battle plan:

> *Come on, then; we will cross over toward them and let them see us. If they say to us, "Wait there until we come to you," we will stay where we are and not go up to them. But if they say, "Come up to us," we will climb up, because that will be our sign that the Lord has given them into our hands.*
> *(1 Samuel 14:8–10)*

It says a lot about the kind of person Jonathan was. In fact, Jonathan asked God for permission to attack. No enemy was dumb enough to give up his higher position, because it meant that you were giving away your advantage. The Philistines coming down was the least likely scenario. It fell into the same category as: "If tomorrow at 1:32:15 p.m. a crossbreed between a golden retriever and a bulldog wearing a jacket rings my doorbell to collect for the WWF, I will not do it." What Jonathan says is: "God, You must perform a miracle to stop me. If not, I'll get them!" Of course, the most likely thing for the Philistines to say is: "Come up here!!" Jonathan considers that which is most obvious as a sign that God wants to hand him the victory. The miracle does not happen, and Jonathan proceeds to attack. A great string of panic and confusion results. The Lord makes the fear among the Philistines complete by moving the earth. The scene becomes so confusing that the Philistines start to fight each other. And that is how God grants Israel victory that day.

Where did it start? With a man with a special mentality: "You must perform a miracle to stop me. Otherwise, I'll simply pick the most dangerous and difficult path."

Be the first to order

How can the mentality of Jonathan be expressed in our lives? The next time you go to a restaurant, be the first to order and don't pick what the others have chosen. Don't change your opinion; stand behind your conviction. Dare to say yes or no when necessary. Let go of your urge to perform, and develop an eye for people. Start resisting peer pressure. Row against the current. Finally, have that difficult conversation with your father, your wife, your son, or your daughter. Choose the hardest path and don't give indolence and laziness a chance to take root. Take responsibility for widows and orphans in the world, and make a difference in the battle against poverty. Or, join a human rights organization that wants to free children from slavery. The mentality of Jonathan can be expressed in our lives in countless ways.

Live like musketeers

For centuries, God has been looking for men who consider it an honour to give their life in service to the King.

Do musketeers still exist?

Are there still men like Gideon, Shammah, and Jonathan?

After a rough trip to the top of the mountain, each of these three heroes left their hessian sack behind. The time of postponing, giving up, and choosing the easiest path was over. These were three men who had the power to serve, to give, to take responsibility, and to make sacrifices.

If we take the quest seriously, if we truly want to answer the invitation of Jesus to take part in that global mission, if we want to become proverbial in "our thing" and wish to powerfully interpret that rock that God has placed on our hearts, we need to live like these three.

Gideon started his mission in spite of his fears. Shammah embodied perseverance and fought for home. Jonathan learned to love the most difficult path.

Now, it's our turn.

Begin. Persevere. Choose the path of the greatest resistance. And then...

Don't give up. Keep going.

9

Red-handed

"Then," said d'Artagnan, letting his arm fall with discouragement, "it is useless to struggle longer. I may as well blow my brains out, and all will be over."

"That's the last folly to be committed," said Athos, "seeing it is the only one for which there is no remedy."

"But I can never escape," said d'Artagnan, "with such enemies."

ALEXANDRE DUMAS

Food is important to many men. "The way to a man's heart is through his stomach" is a well-known proverb. However, many men don't love food enough. Take Jesus, for instance. He was killed over His eating habits. Time after time, we see Him eating with angels, with prostitutes, with Nazis, with Pharisees, with friends. Jesus ate often. And probably too much. Others called Him a glutton. And a drunk. More than 15 Gospel stories centre on a meal. Even in His lessons, Jesus often talks about food, and in many of His parables, a meal takes an important place.

During the meal is when it happens.

In John 21, we read about the last breakfast that Jesus enjoyed with His friends. Seven of the original twelve disciples had travelled from Jerusalem to Galilee, and they decided to spend the night fishing at the lake. All night long, they caught nothing, but most of them weren't thinking about fishing anyway. It was a time of crisis. The world of the disciples had been shaken up in every way possible. The tragedy of the loss, the excitement of the resurrection... it was all too much. The group of friends around Jesus had fallen apart. Seven of them find themselves on the lake this night. Judas has committed suicide, and we don't know the whereabouts of the remaining four.

Circles on the lake

What are these men doing in Galilee, in the north of Israel? Before He died, Jesus had often said, "After my death, I will see you at the mountain, our mountain, in Galilee. The mountain." All members of the band of brothers knew exactly which place Jesus was referring to. They had to go to the mountain, where they would meet Jesus again. Jesus knew that turbulent times were upon them and that despondency and aimlessness were lurking around the corner. He knew that He needed to restore the unity of the group.

And the focus on their mission.

The seven are in Galilee. But not on the mountain. They are sailing on the lake. They have travelled a great distance in the right direction. They had started. They had chosen the path of the most resistance. They had participated in the mission of Jesus. But they had quit too soon. They had given up on their quest. Maybe they took a quick look on the mountain and had failed to find Jesus. They didn't feel like staying on the mountain, so they returned to the lake. They went back to their old fishing circle... and caught nothing.

We've all seen this before. Sailing circles across the lake of Galilee, the empty nets, the old habits, the old patterns, the old emptiness, and now, after everything, after three years of following Jesus and after the two encounters with the Resurrected Lord over the past days... after everything, the disciples go back to fishing. And they catch nothing. Everything is back to normal. It seems as if the past three years have been futile. Old patterns, old pitfalls, old emptiness, the old life.

Where are you right now? On the mountain? Or on the lake? Are you still on your quest? Or did you quit?

Our story

Suddenly, there is a voice. It is Jesus (but the disciples don't know that yet). He wants to have breakfast with his friends. Why? Jesus knows that we tend to settle for the lake, in view of the mountain. He knows that we can sometimes give up and fail to achieve our goals. He knows before we do that we have picked up our hessian sack and sailed in our old circles across the lake of Galilee. Endlessly, the same, the same pitfalls, the empty net syndrome. The old tantrum. The old uncleanness. Your 80-hour work weeks. Your greed. Your fear. Your fleeing from the storms. Your running from responsibilities. Your postponing. Your giving up at home. Your slipping into the path of the least resistance. Your lack of focus on the mission. It is like you haven't changed at all, and because you don't know any better, you return to fishing. That is our story. We encounter Jesus. And other men. We go on an adventure and want to live properly. But after a couple of months or a couple of years, we reach this point. You need a good breakfast.

Cut off

The truth is that we have been cut off from life. We have been cut off from each other. We can attend the most beautiful services or concerts, with thousands of others, and still feel lonely. I (Henk) was talking about friendship once, and a man sighed to me: "Friendship, yes. That's beautiful. We may all be brothers and sisters, but friendship, that's something different." It was an expression of sadness. We know the desire for unity, but we also feel alone. Once, I was called about a man who had attacked his wife. That night, we were talking. I asked him whether he had someone he could talk to. A friend. "No," he replied. "I have nobody." There was so much tragic truth in this one person – the loneliness, the usurpation by life, and the inability to deal with and love one another. We are cut off from each other.

We have also been cut off from creation. We spend most of our lives indoors. We work in heated or air-conditioned offices. We drive in heated or air-conditioned cars. We live in heated or air-conditioned homes. And we hardly get out any more. We are no longer in touch with the beauty of creation. Car manufacturers know this. Think about how often commercials are made in which we see vehicles that take us back to nature, 4×4. These commercials lead us to believe that when we drive that SUV, with those clothes and that appearance (and eating a Snickers bar), we'll be at one with nature again.

It is one of the strengths of The 4th Musketeer. You spend an entire weekend outside. After half a day, you start to feel it: being outside is wonderful. After a couple of days, it doesn't matter whether it rains or the sun shines. You can handle it. You enjoy it. New energy, new odours, new dynamics rush through your veins. God gave us a garden as a house. He didn't give us a tree house. He gave us trees, flowers, bushes.

We are not just cut off from each other and from nature, but we have also been cut off from ourselves. A while ago, I (Henk) was talking to a man. He is extremely successful in what he does, and his company is doing well. Until about a month or two ago, he didn't want to have anything to do with God. He lived for his success. During a 4th Musketeer CSS in the Scottish highlands, he converted. He said, "Over the past few years, I saw nothing and felt nothing. I lived life at 110 miles per hour. Often literally. I wasn't thinking. I was only focusing on my work. Now that I have found Jesus, I am open and interested. I suddenly see things that I never saw before. My emotional life is much richer; my emotions manifest themselves. I can cry again."

But, more than anything else, we have been cut off from Jesus again.

The events at the lake of Galilee remind us of that. The disciples sail on the lake with their empty nets. Jesus calls from the shore and asks them whether they have caught anything. Nobody recognizes His voice.

We have the tendency to forget what the voice of Jesus sounds like.

Subsequently, Jesus asks the seven disciples to throw their nets out on the right side of the boat. A year and a half ago, Jesus told them to do exactly the same. But it doesn't ring a bell with any of the crew.

We simply forget how Jesus works and what He asks from us.

Then, Jesus performs a miracle. He provides them with a net full of splashing fish. This wasn't the first miraculous catch the disciples witnessed. It was at least the second one. But even now, there is nobody who has that "a-ha" moment.

We have the shocking habit of forgetting God's miracles in our lives.

That is our story.

We have survived so many adventures. God has saved us so many times. He has given us such special people in our lives. And still, we lose our courage so quickly. We give up and surrender to fatalistic mumbo jumbo. When that happens, we need a friend who will whisper the truth in our ears.

Caught

Suddenly, John sees it, feels it. How could he be so blind? Goosebumps... from head to toe. Without looking up, he nudges Peter and says, while shuddering, "Peter, it is the Lord!"

Sometimes, a friend has to tell you that, in the things that are happening in your life, you are dealing with none other than Jesus.

Peter jumps overboard. The six other disciples sail to the shore. They arrive simultaneously and stop when they reach the land. This is sacred ground. The seven are entering a temple, because God is there.

What happens then is so real. Jesus wants to have breakfast with his friends. He wants to look them in the eye and share from heart to heart. He has made a fire, with bread and a fish hanging above it. What do the disciples do?

Nothing.

They just stand there. Nobody says a word. They are just playing a little with their feet in the sand and a lowered gaze, waiting for someone to take the initiative. How does a servant behave at the meal of the King? Jesus is the one who breaks the silence. "Can you hand me a couple of fish, so that we'll have enough for everyone?"

Oh, yeah, the fish! They hadn't even landed them. All the fish were still splashing in the water. Peter startles himself awake and – by himself – drags the net with 153 big fish and hundreds of little fish onto the land. Peter is strong. He hands a couple of fish to Jesus. The others watch in silence.

Jesus places the fish on the fire and turns the bread. The disciples don't move. Jesus looks over His shoulder and speaks encouraging words: "Come." Mechanically, the seven start to move and sit down, invited by Jesus.

"Eat something," Jesus urges them. But nobody moves, even though these men had eaten with Jesus hundreds of times, and even though, according to Jewish custom, you can start eating when there are at least two people at the table. You don't even need to wait for the prayer. But this morning, everything is different. Nobody moves a finger and the Bible explicitly says, "Jesus gave them bread." The friends accept the bread and chew it in silence. Nobody takes a fish. So, Jesus gives them fish.

What a breakfast! The disciples are afraid. They feel that they have been caught red-handed in their disbelief, seen in their infidelity, known in their weakness. While Jesus had asked them to come to the mountain, they went fishing on the lake and caught nothing. They felt that they had been discovered in their emptiness... their forgetting of Jesus and everything that He represented. Do you know that feeling? That, in your weakest moment, confronted with the empty net syndrome, you get caught? Jesus, or your wife, or your boss, or your friend, should have found you on the mountain, but instead He finds you on the lake. How do you explain? What is there to say? The seven feel ashamed. Would Jesus have waited for them on the mountain and looked for them when He didn't find them there?

New fire

But, more than anything else, the seven friends are overwhelmed. Because Jesus, the creator of heaven and earth, the destroyer who has crushed the head of the snake, who has personally beaten death and has ransacked the realm of the dead; Jesus, who has broken the power of sin, who is worshipped by millions of angels, and has risen from the dead, makes *fire* here, on our earth.

It doesn't get any better than this.

Jesus makes fire. That is Jesus; he is the big fire-starter. What about your inner fire? Is the passion still burning like it used to? Is the coal still smouldering? Or would you say that the fire is out completely? If so, meet the divine bellows at breakfast: Jesus, the big fire-starter.

That is what happens during the breakfast. Jesus wants to spend time with you and to stir up the fire inside you. You have been through a lot, but the best is yet to come. Your biggest victories, your most wondrous adventures, your best love... it is all ahead of you. Don't think that you're too old, or too weak, or too small. Jesus wants to eat with you, in the presence of friends. He wants to reinforce your heart and give you new fire.

Details are important

And that's not all. Can you see him squatting by the fire? Jesus, who controls galaxies and is preparing a new heaven and a new earth, is focusing on pitta bread and a fish. He prevents them from burning. Jesus, who is responsible for the most dazzling mega projects, is focused on the details of our concern. A crispy bun tastes better than a burnt one. That is Jesus. He isn't only focusing on big, heavenly matters, with theology and complex questions; no, He is focusing on us here, and on the details of our care. That is what you can experience during a meal with the Lord.

The miracle of God's encouragement

And then, the best part comes. Jesus says: "Hey, can you give me some of that fish that *you* caught?" Excuse me? Who had provided that fish? Who had given them that fish? The disciples had hardly anything to do with catching those fish. They had only reeled in their nets. But that is Jesus: He gives, and He hands out. He gives us 153 big fish, and much more, and with that He makes us important. He gives us a meaningful role. He assures us that we are necessary by providing us with enough food. Our gifts, our talents, our money, our being, our energy... it is all part of the abundance that Jesus has provided in our empty nets.

We sometimes wonder why God isn't doing more. Why is He making breakfast with just one fish and one bread? He is God, isn't He? Why isn't He performing more miracles? Why aren't there more divine interventions? When we think like that, we miss the miracle of God's encouragement to us: We can share our 153 fish. We have nothing that we didn't receive from Him. We can't give anything that hasn't been given to us first by Him.

Strength for your mission

That is a breakfast with Jesus. While you're being attacked by enemies, you'll fall back for a moment to put your cards on the table. You can show your despondency and anxiety. You can be discovered, right where you are. He knows you have forgotten about Him. He knows you no longer think about Him. He knows that you're back to sailing in circles, even though you've been through so much with Him. He knows it all, and He invites you. He wants to give you new fire. He wants to feed you to give you strength for your mission, and He wants to encourage you by working together.

When breakfast was finished, Jesus focused on Peter. This tough warrior had denied Jesus three times, several weeks earlier. At a fire. After his resurrection, Jesus paid Peter a visit to restore the relationship. But the boldness and courage had not yet been restored. This morning, Jesus brings Peter back to the fire. And asks him three times: "Do you love me?" Peter knows exactly what Jesus means and starts crying. When you have publicly failed, it is good to see yourself publicly restored. In the presence of his best friends, Peter shows his true colours and Jesus leads him to a sort of revisited experience of his earlier betrayal. Psychologically speaking, it is a both brilliant and necessary move by Jesus. Without this moment, Peter would have been fishing for the rest of his life. On the lake, that is. And Jesus' plans with Peter went far beyond this lake, as beautiful as it was. Peter would preach and lead several congregations. He would be the foundation of the first congregation, and eventually he would – together with his wife – be martyred in honour of Jesus. To follow Jesus that freely, you must be free of blame. And guilt. Peter had already been forgiven. Here, at this breakfast, he is freed of the burden he carried with him. Freed in order to be able to follow.

Do you need recovery?

Is there a painful conversation that you should have with Jesus?

In the presence of several good friends?

Revelation 3:20 is one of the most famous texts from the Bible:

> *Here I am! I stand at the door and knock. If anyone hears my voice and opens the door, I will come in and eat with that person, and they with me.*

See. Suddenly, there He is, at the lakeshore. "When someone hears my voice." That is not so obvious for us, who forget so easily and so often. Hearing Jesus' voice is not so easy in a world that's buried under unnecessary noise. And the door opens. It requires courage. Reluctantly. A little frightened. Because you have been discovered. And most of us have a difficult time with painful conversations. "I will come in." Oh, bliss! "And we will eat together." Jesus will restore us. Or stir us up, even. He will give us food, so that we can resume life with renewed strength. He will point us back to the central mission and discuss the topics that need to be discussed. He will take us further along in our journey from boy to man. Have you forgotten what Jesus thinks of you? "This is my beloved Son, in whom I am well pleased."

I with Him. And He with me.

3

EMPTYING THE HESSIAN SACK

Do musketeers still exist?

The call was clear. The heavenly invitation to take part in that earthly mission couldn't be missed. Imagine that you chose adventure. You got into the right ship and decided to have faith in a sleeping Jesus. You longed to hunt like Nimrod, to become proverbial in your thinking. You devoted yourself to developing the skills of Gideon, Shammah, and Jonathan.

But then...

Suddenly, you found yourself back on the lake. Once again, sailing in the same old circles. The old emptiness.

Fortunately, the great Fire-starter emerged. You found recovery. You were allowed to go once more.

Now what?

How do you prevent Jesus from having to pick you up again tomorrow? What is the key to perseverance?

Emptying your hessian sack.

The contents of the hessian sack make your journey heavy and cause you to quit. And the bull also weighs you down.

Say goodbye to the potatoes – to the old patterns, the urge to have control, lust, the lack of healthy thinking, the fleeing from pain, bitterness, disappointment, the focus on personal success.

How?

On top of the mountain, the boy was alone. No potatoes. No bull. No raven. Free.

That is where we're headed.

10

The statement of Jacob

*"Decidedly, my dear Athos," said d'Artagnan, "I
should like better not to risk anything."*
*"That's a pity," said Athos, coolly. "The
Englishman is overflowing with pistoles. Good
Lord, try one throw! One throw is soon made!."'*
"And if I lose?"
"You will win."
"But if I lose?"

ALEXANDRE DUMAS

They stand before us on the banks of the river. Wearing
shorts. Dirty. They don't know what's about to happen to
them. The assignment is simple. "Walk 500 yards through
the water. Against the current. Let's see how far you'll
get." This is the Jabbok struggle. It is the confrontation
with "the Jacob" inside us. The struggle against the
river current is exhausting. Men come out of the water
stumbling, sometimes even crying. The Jabbok struggle
has impact.

Routing

The very first XCC of The 4th Musketeer took place in the Belgian Ardennes. On one long 72-hour day, 88 men travelled through a beautiful area for a physical test, which, in the end, would turn out to be a spiritual journey. The purpose of the journey was to bring the men to the core of their love of God, to their loved ones, and to themselves. And it was gruelling. At the end of the first 24 hours, most men were completely exhausted. Some of them withdrew and fell silent. Others used their last bit of energy to express their displeasure in a way that suits a rugged area. And others rested, wrapped in their rescue blankets, naked and shivering. The bivouac at the end of the first 24 hours was like a battlefield. Every man fought, sometimes against God, but mostly against themselves. Then, the sun came up and the journey continued. After a string of mental and physical challenges, the journey ended in a climax at the base of the cross. Men were crying. Men were praying. Men came home.

"You don't know what's coming"

What made the first XCC so impressive? We spoke with the men afterwards. And they all said: "You don't know what's coming, which makes it a mentally tough challenge. At least at home, you have the comfort of waking up with the idea that you're in control of your own agenda, that you can decide what the day will be like, and that you have some control over your life. That feeling is gone during an XCC. In the few hours that you sleep, you can only wake up with the feeling that you have reached an unpredictable and dangerous chapter in your life. To-do lists won't work.

Nothing works. The only thing that works is being alert, allowing the adrenaline to do the work, and assessing your responses, minute by minute. You don't know what's coming, and that makes it intense."

The unparalleled effect of the journey wasn't so much caused by the physical elements, nor by the 72-hour duration, and not even by the rain and the cold. It was caused by giving up control. And men don't like that. Not being in control, being dragged along in a stream that happens to have the strongest current; we don't like that. We want to make life work in our favour. We want control.

One illustration of the desire to control is the way that some participants had prepared for the third edition of the XCC. Men had used the weapon of the Internet to eliminate as many ambiguities about the programme as possible. Testimonials from previous participants on The 4th Musketeer website and photos on YouTube had been used to gather as much information as possible. Google Earth came in handy to identify possible routes and to predict the likely course of the programme. That is how many men started the physical and mental journey: with a definite idea and a mental roadmap of what was likely to happen. They started with a sense of having some control over what was going to happen. It appeared to be enough to prevent them from embarking on the adventure without being completely disoriented and from ending without being completely broken. It proved to make the difference between a "gruelling" and just a "very intense" XCC. The XCC tells us a lot about ourselves. Men want to be in control and are resourceful enough to seize that control.

Jacob, the gripper

Someone who also loved grip and control was Jacob. Jacob was the man who grabbed and didn't let go, the man that you had to pass twice, the man who was continually trying to get a grip on life. It started as early as in the womb. Jacob wanted to rule over his twin brother and to be stronger than him. But that proved to be very difficult. With their struggles, they drove their mother Rebecca to insanity. The two boys struggled so hard against each other inside her womb that it brought her to despair: "Why is this happening to me?" (Genesis 25:22)

Ultimately, Jacob had to succumb. Esau was the first one to be born. The most that Jacob could gain was to grab the heel of his twin brother. That was how he emerged. As a reward, he was given the name Jacob, "the heel gripper" – like a wrestler who makes a sneaky manoeuvre to win the match in the end. It was symbolic of the rest of his life. He lost the initial battle at birth, but he didn't surrender. He had to be the first one, the superior of his brother, whatever it took. He had to gain the respect, the honorary position of the firstborn... by using his elbows if necessary. And thus he pursued the rights of the firstborn. In this, he cunningly used Esau's temperament.

Jacob wants to be the first

Esau was everything that Jacob wasn't. Jacob was calm and homely. Esau was the adventurer, the outdoor type – the man who loved open fields, the outdoor life, the hunt; the man who lived for the prey of the day, for the wild game, and for his father. Initially, the ruddy Esau was the "diamond in the rough" type of person. But, as he grew up into manhood, he lost more and more of his spiritual sensitivity, his sexual cleanliness and strength, and his vision of what is holy and good. And when the time had come, Jacob struck like a predator who finally saw his chance. The starved Esau fell for the trap of the delicious food and threw the right of being the firstborn before his brother's feet. Jacob seized the opportunity and won. Jacob wanted to be the first, and he got what he wanted.

Jacob wants the best part

But Jacob wanted more. He didn't only want to have front-row seats; he wanted the best seat as well. Jacob wanted the blessing of his father. And that wasn't an easy thing to obtain. It was more than just the regards of an email signature. The blessing was the double part, the best part. The blessing meant the passing on of the torch, the passing on authority, continuing the pursuit of a destination. Jacob wanted his father's blessing as reassurance that he would be fine. He and his parents already knew that God had promised him that blessing. Still, he had decided to lend God a hand, because, you never know. He used every trick in the book to mislead his father, Isaac. On the advice of his mother, Jacob pretended to be his brother, deceived his blind father, and seized the blessing. Jacob wanted the best part and got what he wanted.

Jacob wants to open the door a little

Esau was furious, and Jacob had to run. When God appeared before Jacob in a dream in Bethel, Jacob was extremely impressed. Very carefully, Jacob considered the idea that the God of his grandfather and the God of his father might one day be his God as well. He made a calculated promise. There could be room for God in his heart, but only if God did exactly what was asked of Him.

Jacob wants the most beautiful woman

Jacob moved on and ended up with his Uncle Laban. Jacob fell head over heels in love with the beautiful Rachel. He desired her. He wanted her. He wanted her more than he had wanted anything in his life. And Jacob started doing the maths. According to the law back then, Laban could not possibly marry off his second daughter before his first one was married. Jacob knew that he would confront Laban with a dilemma if he were to ask for the hand of his youngest daughter. And that is why Jacob made Laban an offer that he couldn't refuse: "I'll work for you seven years in return for your younger daughter Rachel." (Genesis 29:18)

Laban couldn't let this deal slide, and so he effortlessly broke the customs of his time and agreed. Jacob wanted the most beautiful woman, and he got what he wanted.

Jacob wants freedom

After Jacob had worked for Laban for 20 years, he secretly left with all his possessions and his entire family, which consisted of four women and a lot of children. Jacob "stole the heart" of Laban, the author of the book of Genesis says, a statement with which the author expresses his disapproval in a way that is rare for the book of Genesis. But Jacob's wife and children weren't simply his possessions. He shared authority with Laban. By leaving without Laban's permission, Jacob risked a war within the family. Still, he left. Jacob wanted freedom, seized it Jacob-style, and got what he wanted.

Jacob wants to secure his life

Then, it was time for the most difficult task to date: surviving the reunion with Esau. On his way back to Canaan, an encounter with his brother was inevitable. For 20 years, Esau had been able to build up his hatred towards his brother. For all those years, Jacob had feared this day. He anxiously tried to get a grip on his brother once again. He sent him messengers and tried to calm his brother down, mainly by stressing that Esau is his lord and Jacob is but his servant, although the theft of the right of the firstborn has caused the opposite to be true. In addition, he hinted that he was willing to buy Esau's forgiveness with the many possessions he had gathered. And then, when Jacob was at the end of his possibilities, with his back against the wall, seeing no way out and feeling condemned to death, he started praying.

That's how these things go.

After his "amen", Jacob continued to calculate. He divided his people and cattle into two groups. If Esau killed one group, the other could escape, and vice versa. Genius. In addition, he made a brilliant move, in which he cleverly used the power of repetition. He subdivided 580 head of cattle into five groups, managed by five servants. At intervals, he sent the gifts to his brother, one by one. That was safer than one big gift. He could imagine his brother angrily rejecting a single gift. Then, he would have a problem. Five gifts were safer and smarter. With each gift, Esau would calm down a little more, helped by Jacob's servants repeating the refrain

"This is from Jacob, your servant, for Esau, my Lord." He could do nothing but hope it worked.

The statement of Jacob

Promises, prophecies, dreams, direct revelations, divine interventions, armies of angels – nothing helped.

Jacob kept grabbing. He kept living according to "the statement of Jacob":

"If I don't take care of myself, who will?"

"Nobody."

Hence, "Jacob".

And that was why he grabbed the heel of his brother, the right of the firstborn, the blessing, the most beautiful woman, his freedom, why he did anything he could to survive the encounter with his brother. He grabbed to get what he wanted. He wanted to be the first; he wanted to matter. He wanted the best part, and he wanted the guarantee of a good life. He wanted beauty and the satisfaction that comes with it. He wanted freedom, and he wanted to escape from someone else's authority. He wanted to secure his life and escape death.

Jacob grabbed because, "If I don't take care of myself, who will?" It was the statement of Jacob. What did it lead to? Five times, Jacob tried to get things his own way. And five times, he got into nothing but trouble.

What the statement of Jacob leads to

He became the first and got the best part, but he never saw his father and mother again. He got the most beautiful woman and found satisfaction, but then he got three more women and a lot of jealousy, arguments, and domestic tension along with it. He got his freedom, but he cut it very close. If God hadn't intervened by means of a dream to Laban, this action would have been his downfall. And not only his.

And now, right before the encounter with Esau, he causes trauma to his family. Seeing your father walk around in agony and despair, as fair game, desperately searching for a way out, really affects you as a son. There is significant tension. They are facing death. Four hundred murderous men are on their way to take revenge, and a bloodbath seems inevitable. Or at least, that's what Jacob thinks. Then, he does the last thing he can do. He brings his wife and children and possessions to relative safety, across the river.

And then, after all of those frantic calculations and all of those attempts for control, a brief sentence ultimately expresses where a control freak ends up: "Jacob was left alone" (Genesis 32:24a).

All alone.

Ending up all alone is the danger for every man. Because, just like Jacob, we grab, we control, and we spasmodically try to be free. The first row is not enough, we also want the best seat, the most beautiful woman, ultimate freedom, and a safe life. We insure ourselves to the bone, we avoid all risks, we treat our kids as clay, and we often also believe that we can slap a label onto God. We say that we want to be musketeers in the service of the King, but do we really want that? We'd rather be the king instead. We hate our distance from the throne. We feel that making all decisions by ourselves would be better for all parties. And then, the Bible adds: "Do not worry about tomorrow" (Matthew 6:34).

Everything inside of us is fighting this. It's what we're so good at. We eagerly tend to seize beyond our power. And when we get up on our toes and still can't reach it, we keep trying until we can. We think that what we have is the result of our own personal efforts. We feel that it isn't up to God, but up to us, to protect what we have. We don't share with others, but we keep to ourselves, because you never know whether you'll have enough tomorrow.

The tragedy of many men

If we don't watch our steps, we'll stay behind, disillusioned. All alone. It is the tragic end for many men. How is this possible? You want to do things exactly your way, and moreover, you want to do them really well. To you, that is much more important than developing healthy relationships with the people you love. You feel anger and annoyance building up when things don't go the way you want them to. You find it more and more difficult to suppress a critical attitude towards others. You're not aware of it, but you are inevitably starting to get stuck in your habits. More and more often, you use intimidation and manipulation as tools to turn situations to your favour and to get what you want. Add all of these things up, and the outcome is:

You are all alone. Cut off from yourself, from your loved ones, from a life in openness and free from pain. Cut off from the joyous life with God.

The gripper grabbed

It is important to be aware of the fact that, when we have control issues, we actually have issues with God Himself.

This is where Jacob is now. At the deepest level, he has no issues with Esau, but he does have an issue with God. Is there any hope left for Jacob? Can a man stop that habit of endlessly calculating? He can, but it requires an intervention from God: "a man wrestled with him till daybreak" (Genesis 32:24b).

A man needs to first struggle with God Himself. He will only feel his weakness in a direct confrontation with the Invincible. The gripper must first be grabbed himself. And in that process of being grabbed, a man discovers that God can't be manipulated. That is where a man reaches the end of his strength. Instead of struggling with life, it is important for a man to learn how to struggle with God. Just like Jacob.

And a question is introduced at the end of the struggle: "What is your name?" (Genesis 32:27)

Who are you, really? The question touches Jacob in the depths of his soul. The pain of the nagging memories of the bitter outcry of Esau cuts through his wounded heart for the thousandth time. There's a reason why his name is Jacob. Impostor. Who are you, really? By giving his name, Jacob gives himself. To God. Lonely. Exhausted. Tired of fighting.

Reborn

A Musketeer who participated in an XCC in the Belgian Ardennes tells about his Jabbok struggle in a river:

> An experience that turned my life upside down
> was the Jabbok struggle. First, we read the
> history from the Bible. Then, we prayed with our
> group. Then, exhausted from the previous days,
> we went up against the flowing river. During

the Jabbok struggle, we were all in it together, but it was also every man for himself. Man, nature, and God. Together in the river, but only struggling with the water. Sometimes, the water was knee deep, and sometimes it was up to our chest. Sometimes we staggered. Men fell, and then got back on their feet, helped by brothers or crawling up by themselves. When I staggered, I looked for something to grip, and I grabbed an overhanging branch. It snapped. Then, I realized that my grip was not on this branch or other things that I could hold onto. I had the grip in my other hand, being the Bible. While struggling, I saw the image that I was fighting against a few cubic yards of water and that my strength stands in no proportion to the strength and greatness of God. Of Him, who has created rivers, seas, and oceans. It was here that I let go of my own will and surrendered myself to God. It was here that I experienced a deep touch of God, who carried me from then on. From this moment forward, the water was no longer ice cold, and the fatigue was no longer a problem. Here, in this river, I was baptized by the water and in the Spirit of God. Despite how tough this struggle was, I came out of the river reborn.

And Peter, another Musketeer, tells about his physical struggle with men during an XCC in the Scottish Highlands:

I have Tourette's syndrome. During the weekend, I found out that I have been struggling with wanting to be someone else for 35 years. I don't want to respond the way I usually respond. I just want to be normal and not so complicated.

Later on in the weekend, we had to physically battle each other as teams, in a circle marked by ropes. There, I physically experienced my struggle of the past 35 years. Twice, I was thrown out of the circle. The first time, I lasted for a long while, but the second time, I was out before I knew it. When I was thrown out of the circle, it felt like a liberation from my struggle. I felt that I no longer have to battle my giant, because I have been freed from it.

There, in Scotland, I found out that God loves me the way I am and that I am perfect the way I am. I felt like: I am Tourette. But now, I realized that I AM Peter and I HAVE Tourette. I don't have to struggle anymore.

Struggling with God makes you a different person. Jacob emerged out of the river reborn as well, because God had given him a new name: "Your name will no longer be Jacob, but Israel [warrior of God]." (Genesis 32:28)

The struggle with God turns an impostor into a warrior of God.

The sun comes up: a new beginning

Jacob has changed. How? He dares to take risks, because God protects him. As soon as Esau appears with his 400 men, it says: "He himself went on ahead." (Genesis 33:3)

In addition, he starts giving generously, because he realizes that everything he has originates from God. To Esau, he says:

"Please accept the present that was brought to you, for God has been gracious to me and I have all I need." (Genesis 33:11)

And Jacob grows fond of the Lord. Once he is back in Canaan, he builds an altar, which he calls "El is the God of Israel".

For 20 years, Jacob had been terrified to run into Esau again, only to discover that his brother had long ago forgiven him. What a waste of energy! All those years could have been lived so differently.

You don't have to be a Jacob forever. You can be Israel.

You don't have to force your way through life. You can live an uninhibited life.

You don't have to grab. You can receive.

You don't have to remain as a boy with a hessian sack. You can be free.

11

The theological significance of the ostrich

Arrived at the staircase, it was still worse. There were four Musketeers on the bottom steps, amusing themselves with the following exercise, while ten or twelve of their comrades waited upon the landing place to take their turn in the sport.

One of them, stationed upon the top stair, naked sword in hand, prevented, or at least endeavoured to prevent, the three others from ascending.

These three others fenced against him with their agile swords.

D'Artagnan at first took these weapons for foils, and believed them to be buttoned; but he soon perceived by certain scratches that every weapon was pointed and sharpened, and that at each of these scratches not only the spectators, but even the actors themselves, laughed like so many madmen.

ALEXANDRE DUMAS

The Adventures of Tom Sawyer and *The Adventures of Huckleberry Finn* are two of the best "men books" ever written. Some people discard these books as "boy books", but in doing so, they don't give these precious stories about the naughty Tom and Huck the credit that they deserve. Both books invite us to live life to the fullest. The most hilarious scene is the one in which Tom, Huck, and Joe have decided to live the pirate life on an island in the Mississippi River. Before long, a search is initiated to find the boys. From their hiding place, the boys see that a ship is firing cannons, in an attempt to make their – possibly drowned – bodies, float to the surface.

> *They felt like heroes in an instant. Here was a gorgeous triumph; they were missed; they were mourned; hearts were breaking on their account; tears were being shed; accusing memories of unkindness to these poor lost lads were rising up, and unavailing regrets and remorse were being indulged; and best of all, the departed were the talk of the whole town, and the envy of all the boys, as far as this dazzling notoriety was concerned. This was fine. It was worthwhile to be a pirate, after all.*

Tom and his friends manage to maximize the tragedy of their disappearance: they remain hidden on the island for several days, and on Sunday, they attend their own funeral, where they witness their own memorial, and in the supreme moment, they march forward as brothers. Three dead pirates, more alive than ever.

Playing is essential

Various game theories argue that by playing people learn, relax, can vent their energy, or become stimulated in their creativity. In a study, people were asked – for one day – to refrain from doing anything that felt like a game or was not essential. The participants reported that the day without games made them more fatigued, sleepier, less healthy, less relaxed, and less creative. They were more easily annoyed, more easily depressed and distracted, and enjoyed life less. Playing allows people to organize experiences, to find balance (again), and to (re)create.

Various phases are distinguished in the creative process: preparation (you perceive a problem that requires a solution), incubation (you distance yourself from the problem and subconsciously allow it to be absorbed by your system), illumination (the "aha" moment), verification (is the solution you found to the problem correct?), and effect (the consolidation of the solution). The decisive phase in the creative process is the incubation phase: letting go or letting it settle. It is in the moments that you aren't working on the problem that the solution is found. Playing is essential to this. It is an excellent way to distance yourself, to open your senses, and to receive a revelation. With us, solutions or breakthroughs often emerge while running, or during a good conversation with a friend. Relaxation and playing has a positive effect on the creative, creating ability in your life. There's a reason why the climax of God's creation, man, was the result of a creative initiative: "Let's..."

The pure joy of a 62-year-old

Recently, we had a preparation day for a new XCC weekend. Eighty men had gathered at the agreed coordinates. The teams were given various assignments, including capturing their team flag. The team flags were defended by the Musketeer supervisor up on a hill, somewhere in the forest. The team members were all given a ribbon around their arm and had to use their ingenuity and violence to steal their flag from the hill. When one of the supervisors pulled the ribbon from their arm, they had to cease and desist. Prior to this assignment, we had focused extensively on a set of warm-up exercises, during which a lot of attention was paid to the abs and arm muscles. One of the participants who stood out for me was a tall 62-year-old man. He had signed up for the weekend all by himself. The push-ups and the running were hard for him. He grunted and moaned, and I thought to myself: "Please don't collapse." However, he didn't give up, and I persevered. I walked up to him and told him not to force himself. He didn't want to hear it. He loved the fact that he had to suffer.

The capture-the-flag event was pretty rough. Teams used their long wooden beams like battering rams, bodies crashed into each other, men were thrown onto the ground, and there was some serious fighting. The gloves were off. Blood was the limit, which, according to some, was far too soft! A randomly passing mountain biker stopped and looked baffled as he watched the battle going on. Running guys, wrestling bodies, torn clothes, stealthy silhouettes – get your act together. But then, the faces of all those 80 men – faces of directors, pastors, office clerks and commercial men, teachers and commandos, fathers and grandfathers – all those faces lit up. This was pure joy, happening right here. And, as I was on the hill to throw men onto the ground and rob them of their ribbons, I saw a grey-haired man flashing by in the corner of my eye. He had appeared from out of nowhere and had rushed past our defences. The 62-year-old grabbed the flag and waved it triumphantly. The smirk on his face, the glow in his eyes, the powerful waving of the flag; this was grand. I am certain that his wife reaped the fruits of his victory, and that the days of muscle aches did nothing but remind him of his victory.

The dark side of playing

Of course, playing is not always a positive experience. It can also have a destructive, irresponsible side, as Chuck Palahniuk depicts in his dark novel *Fight Club*. Brad Pitt and Edward Norton play the lead character, Tyler Durden, in the movie version of the book. On one hand, Tyler (as portrayed by Edward Norton) is a fine white-collar employee at an insurance company. On the other hand, Tyler is angry at the system and angry at the impossibility of living as a man in Western society. Tyler wants to feel that he's alive. He wants to be a warrior. So, together with his alter ego Brad Pitt, he starts Fight Club, a gathering of men who fight on Sunday nights in a dimly lit basement. The fight club soon proves to be a success. Hundreds, and later even thousands of men secretly measure their strength and then appear at work on Monday, covered with bruises and scratches. In a memorable scene from the movie, Brad Pitt rants about the background of the initiative for the fight club, in a shady basement, in the presence of dozens of men:

> *Man, I see in fight club the strongest and*
> *smartest men who've ever lived. I see all of this*
> *potential, and I see squandering. I see an entire*
> *generation pumping gas, waiting tables; slaves*
> *with white collars. Advertising has us chasing*
> *cars and clothes, working at jobs we hate so we*
> *can buy stuff we don't need. We're the middle*
> *children of history, man. No purpose or place.*
> *We have no Great War. No Great Depression.*
> *Our Great War's a spiritual war... our Great*
> *Depression is our lives. We've all been raised*
> *on television to believe that one day we'd all be*
> *millionaires, and movie gods, and rock stars. But*
> *we won't. And we're slowly learning that fact.*
> *And we're very, very pissed off.*

Because of the smallness of their lives and the disappointing realization that they have been misled by the media and commerce regarding the things that truly matter in life, these men decide to fight. They beat each other to a pulp, learn to overcome their fears, and find a purpose in their lives. Similarly, there are men who seek their salvation with partying, alcohol, or women. A man told me (Henk) that, around the age of 45, a divorced father of children had finally found the purpose of his life: women. Women in general. Feeling women, loving women, getting to know women.

Discontent about our insignificant lives is widespread. Sooner or later, everyone discovers that goals such as material things, sex, and money are much too insignificant to spend your whole life on. In the search for more, men often choose "playing" as the first way out. The tragedy of *Fight Club* – and countless men – is not that they're fighting, but that they think that it is their life's purpose. They wanted to live, but they settled for less. They went on a journey, but they quit too soon. And then, playing becomes something evil, something empty and dark.

Live, play, enjoy

The Bible is at least ambivalent in the field of play and joy. Solomon says in Ecclesiastes 2:2: "'Laughter,' I said, 'is madness. And what does pleasure accomplish?'"

And in Proverbs 10:23: "A fool finds pleasure in wicked schemes, but a person of understanding delights in wisdom."

And in Sirach 21:20 (NRSV), the apocryphal equivalent of Proverbs, it states: "A fool raises his voice when he laughs, but the wise smile quietly".

In the Bible, playing and laughing are often addressed with care. A certain detachment from earthly pleasures resonates in texts here and there. But those who want to distance Christianity from these pleasures will be in for a rude awakening. Before all that is serious and grave, God is first and foremost the God of abundance and joy. All of creation is one big jubilee: live, play, enjoy, discover, mine. The huge variety of fish, birds, and animals is an expression of the endless joy of God. Earth laughs in flowers. Each sunrise is another invitation to celebrate life.

The ostrich

It is later, and we have grown up. It is time to play. Meister Eckhardt, an influential late medieval theologian and philosopher, wrote:

> *Truly! Truly! By God! Be as sure of it as you are*
> *that God lives: at the least good deed done here*
> *in this world, the least bit of good will, the least*
> *good desire, all the saints in heaven and on*
> *earth rejoice, and together with the angels their*
> *joy is such that all the joy in this world can't*
> *be compared. But the joy of them all together*
> *amounts to as little as a bean when compared to*
> *the joy of God over good deeds. For truly, God*
> *laughs and plays.*

Truly, God laughs and plays. Human beings and the entire creation are a result of His endless creativity and creative ability. What kind of God would come up with the funny monkey, the jewellery-stealing raven, or the smiley bird (a paradise bird that smiles when he wants to attack an enemy)? What kind of creator builds mountains almost six miles high, when two miles of rock would be an insurmountable obstacle for a mere mortal? What kind of brain comes up with seas that are more than six miles deep, whereas for us people, paddling in knee-deep water would be more than enough? The Bible shows us God, playing with the mythical sea serpent: "There the ships go to and fro, and Leviathan, which you formed to frolic there." (Psalm 104:26)

Later, we can read how God challenges Job to play with the crocodile, and we see how God made the ostrich; happy, big, fast and, at the same time, without the ability to fly. Isn't that a divine joke? Or, what about the colour green? One colour, in more than a million shades, every leaf its own shade of green. There are countless stars. Why are there so many twinkling stars, while we can probably see only about 9,000 with our naked eye? Where is the "theological significance" in that? All those winks, witticisms, and rarities are an expression of the pleasure of God.

An abundance of way too much

God's zest for life is also expressed in the life of Jesus. Jesus had an eye for detail. He saw the sparrows, the birds in the sky, and the lilies in the field. Most of the miracles He performed had a serious undertone and a clear goal. In addition, some miracles show a remarkable kind of playfulness and abundance. Like that time when Jesus made more than 600 quarts of wine for a small farmer's wedding in a small town in Galilee. And the wedding guests had already drunk so much that they could hardly taste what they were drinking. Why? Why so much? And why so much wine?

Or that time when Jesus gave about 20,000 people a free meal. He didn't have to do that. The crowd had followed Him without asking and had disrupted His weekend away with the disciples. The people had walked to Jesus in a couple of hours. In their enthusiastic hurry, they had forgotten to bring lunch, but, if necessary, they could have easily made it home. It may not have been pleasant, but it wasn't life-threatening. The second time that Jesus miraculously multiplied food, it was because of an emergency. The people had been with Him for three days, somewhere in the wilderness. Something had to happen. But this first time, it was optional. Still, Jesus used His divine power to provide a gigantic feast: 20,000 happy men, women, and children, with mouths covered in fish grease. Jesus enjoyed it all. It wasn't necessary. But He did it anyway. Because He loved it.

That is the idea: doing things because they are beautiful, or because they are festive, or just because they are fun.

Capture a flag. Our lives are packed with serious occasions, complex (pastoral) issues, or existential questions. We tell ourselves that we need to spend our time wisely. And wisely means: in such a way that it benefits others. This is too limited a view on life. From time to time, you have to enjoy yourself and play!

There is "a time to weep and a time to laugh, a time to mourn and a time to dance" (Ecclesiastes 3:4).

The importance of laughter

In the fantastic and brilliant novel, *The Name of the Rose*, a number of puzzling murders take place in a Benedictine abbey in North Italy. William and Adso, the main characters of the book, investigate the murders. The search for the cause of the mysterious murders leads them to a manuscript of Aristotle, the great Greek philosopher, which was thought to be lost. The manuscript is about the importance of laughter. Jorge, the former librarian of the renowned library of the abbey, wants to do everything in his power to prevent the contents of this manuscript from being revealed to the monks. He fears that people will discover laughter as a weapon to fight their fears. That is why he has glued the pages of the book together, using a deadly poison. When people want to turn the pages of the book, they will lick their fingers, pick up the poison from the pages, and cause their own death. In the climax of this monumental book, William and Jorge are talking about the importance of laughter in the presence of Adso. Jorge says:

> *Laughter, for a few moments, distracts the villein from fear. But law is imposed by fear, whose true name is the fear of God. This book could strike*

> *the Luciferine spark that would set a new fire to*
> *the whole world, and laughter would be defined*
> *as the new art... for cancelling fear. And what*
> *would we be, we sinful creatures, without fear,*
> *perhaps the most foresighted, the most loving of*
> *divine gifts?*

Laughter frees us from fear for a moment. While the church has preached fear of God for centuries in order to keep the people in check, it is important to develop a balanced picture... based on pleasure, laughter, and playfulness. We have already seen that God plays, and that Jesus sometimes performed miracles in which it seems like He "went a little overboard" and did a little too much in moments that He didn't have to. Another sign of the playfulness of Jesus is His use of humour in conversations with people.

The humour of Jesus

When Jesus compares a rich person entering the kingdom of God with a camel crawling through the eye of a needle, that is humour. We have the tendency to immediately start theologizing and explaining to one another that "the eye of the needle" was the nickname for a small side gate in a big city. A camel that wanted to get in after hours had to take off its entire luggage and slowly move in. Similarly, a rich person has to strip himself of all his riches to enter the kingdom of God. Of course, this explanation is true, but it ignores the subtlety and creativity of Jesus' communication. Because, in Jesus' time, they already had needles as we have come to know them: a pin with a sharp point and an eye for the thread. Chances are that, when hearing "the eye of the needle", Jesus' audience first thought of the eye of a needle instead of a gate. Try imagining a camel crawling through the eye of a needle. It's impossible. And even if it were possible, it's absurd. It would get stuck halfway. That is why there are camels with two humps instead of one.

Jesus used a wealth of similar, humorous speaking styles, such as: extrapolation to the extreme ("when you tell this mountain: 'Move from here to there,' it will move"), the surprise of deceit ("Blessed are those who mourn"), or choosing the most unexpected images or events (a Pharisee who swallows a camel). These are all ways to create surprise, fun, and laughter, forms of communication that Jesus used consistently.

There was never a dull moment with Jesus. He dared to say things that others thought, but never said. He could make complex matters incredibly simple through the use humour. We often read the Gospels as extremely serious books, with nothing but serious conversations regarding life and death. The truth is that the Gospels are packed with the humour and zest for life of Jesus. When I (Henk) was telling this to a group of students, a young woman exclaimed: "I don't believe any of that. Jesus didn't use any humour." I challenged her to put her statement to the test and to read the Gospels through these glasses for the next two weeks: Where did Jesus use humour? Two weeks later, she returned with surprising results. "I began reading Matthew, and I stopped halfway, because it quickly became clear to me. Jesus used humour on every page."

Laughter makes us feel alive

Laughter and play are important, because they significantly improve our quality of life. Solomon says:

So I commend the enjoyment of life, because
there is nothing better for a person under the
sun than to eat and drink and be glad. Then joy
will accompany them in their toil all the days
of the life God has given them under the sun.
(Ecclesiastes 8:15)

Joy gives energy and increases a person's resilience. A study categorized 122 men who had suffered a heart attack, based on a scale from pessimistic to optimistic. Eight years later, the 25 biggest pessimists were compared to the 25 biggest optimists from the random tests. The results were staggering. Of the 25 most pessimistic men, 21 had died. Of the 25 most optimistic men, only 6 had died. That is the power of laughter. You have a 300 per cent chance of living longer. It is better to enjoy containers full of chocolate ice cream than to desperately eat broccoli that you hate.

Embrace play

If Christian life feels somewhat mechanical or has fallen into a practised routine, you might need a good "capture-the-flag" session. If there is an ambience of gloom or fatigue for the things of God around you, like a heavy winter coat, then you need to take an "excess of seriousness" out of your hessian sack and leave it behind you. Find the right balance. Embrace play. You need it to be able to persevere, to serve, to choose the road of the most resistance when it truly matters. You need the power of laughter to prevent yourself from falling back into your old patterns, old habits, old emptiness.

During the XCC weekends, we see a lot of men undergo radical changes due to an intimate encounter with God, with themselves, and with other men. The adventures in nature have a liberating effect on the soul. Laughing and crying together, fighting, resting, and worshipping forges souls together and makes the pores wide open to life.

12

The slaughter of Olaf the Ox

This introduction to Milady Clarik occupied the head of our Gascon greatly. He remembered in what a strange manner this woman had hitherto been mixed up in his destiny. According to his conviction, she was some creature of the cardinal, and yet he felt himself invincibly drawn towards her by one of those sentiments for which we cannot account.

ALEXANDRE DUMAS

If there's anything that can jeopardize our mission, it is this development: from love to lust. We are facing overwhelming forces of nature that play their game inside us. How many men have fallen victim to lust? End of quest. End of participation in that global mission. Great start, but early exit, because love became lust or because lust didn't become anything else than lust. The Greek described lust as "madness of the gods". In Dumas's story, d'Artagnan loses all sense of reality, gives up on his childhood love, and becomes involved in a dangerous flirtation with a deadly woman. Love makes you blind. Lust robs you of all your senses.

What it can lead to?

General Dallaire was the commander of the UN troops during the 1994 genocide in Rwanda. With his 250 men, he had an impossible mission. Between April and August 1994, darkness ruled in Rwanda. Over half a million Tutsis were murdered, often in a horrible way. General Dallaire writes in his memoirs:

> We drove through village after deserted village, some still smouldering. Garbage, rags and bodies intermingled at places where either an ambush or a massacre had occurred. We drove by abandoned checkpoints ringed with corpses, sometimes beheaded and dumped like rubbish, sometimes stacked meticulously beside neat piles of heads. Many corpses rapidly decayed into blinding white skeletons in the hot sun.
>
> For a long time, I completely wiped the death masks of raped and sexually mutilated girls and women from my mind, as if what had been done to them was the last thing that would send me over the edge. But if you looked, you could see the evidence, even in the whitened skeletons. The legs bent and apart. A broken bottle, a rough branch, even a knife between them… and always a lot of blood. But it was the expressions on their dead faces that assaulted me the most, a frozen image of shock, pain and humiliation.

More than 500,000 women were raped over a period of several months, often by men with AIDS – a delayed murder mechanism. The scale of murder and rape in Rwanda was unprecedented. The way this was done also defies the imagination. Parents were forced to kill their children. Parents were forced to watch as the arms and legs and genitals of their children were cut off before they were murdered. People were burnt alive, killed as slowly as possible, tortured. In Hitler's concentration camps, murder was mass destruction. In Rwanda, murder had become a craft.

Why is this so shocking?

Because it didn't happen too long ago? Because so many people were involved? Because "we" from the West didn't do anything and even pulled out our UN forces? Because you're not supposed to commit murder and rape? Yes, that's all true. But the true shock is in the anti-humanity of what happened here. The reign of death.

How is it possible? How can something that was made so beautifully – man – and was imagined so beautifully – sexuality – end up in such an anti-human monstrous massacre?

Sexuality is beautiful

Because, let us be clear on that: There is nothing wrong with sexuality. On the contrary, sex is beauty and has something divine. Sexuality is enchanting, and, ultimately, born in heaven. Our God is a Trinity and from the plurality of God, who is burning passion and overwhelming love, God gave us hints to get to know Him. God gave us the oceans to show us how broad and overwhelming He is. God gave us the mountains to show us that He is reliable and bigger than we can comprehend. God gave us colours to show us that He is creative and diverse. And God gave us sex to allow us to experience the unity, passion, and love that reigns within the Trinity. Because it finds its origin in God Himself, sexuality is an uncontrollable fire.

> *[Love] burns like a blazing fire, like a mighty flame. Many waters cannot quench love; rivers cannot sweep it away. If one were to give all the wealth of one's house for love, it would be utterly scorned. (Song of Songs 8:6b–7)*

These are words of Solomon, from the Song of Songs, a book that is so sensual and sexual that Jewish men were not allowed to read this book before they were 40. Love in the Song of Songs is usually a euphemism for the sexual fusion with one's beloved.

Sexuality is a festival, a celebration of being human. It is a form of play that has a (re)creating effect. It is powerful, because it was concocted in heaven. The divine origin makes sex, in principle, holy, pure, and good.

Perversification

However, we all know that sex has been made banal, grotesque, or degrading in every possible way. In many cases in our world, sex has become a sin. Distorted by self-centredness and self-indulgence, it has become a parody of the true joys that God created. In *The Screwtape Letters*, C.S. Lewis presents a master demon who introduces his student demon to the dark strategies of the devil:

> *Never forget that when we are dealing with any pleasure in its healthy and normal and satisfying*

*form, we are, in a sense, on the Enemy's ground.
I know we have won many a soul through
pleasure. All the same, it is His invention, not
ours. He made the pleasures: all our research so
far has not enabled us to produce one. All we
can do is to encourage the humans to take the
pleasures which our Enemy has produced, at
times, or in ways, or in degrees, which He has
forbidden.*

God created joy, including the enjoyment of beauty and sexuality. Everything the devil does is designed to pull the enjoyments of God from their context and pervert them, so that which was created good will eventually ruin our lives. And can even be used to hurt and to kill others.

How did we get from there to here?

How is it possible that something so divine and so fragile can become so destructive and anti-human? It all has to do with your perspective. And mindset. The Hutus, who slaughtered the Tutsis, no longer considered the Tutsis to be human, to be their brothers and sisters. They had begun thinking in terms of us–them. The Tutsis were cockroaches. They had to be squashed. Everything the Hutus thought and said about their compatriots became thoughts and words in terms of us–them.

Their neighbour became an animal, an animal you could squash.

When we talk about sex, we often use animal terms: he is a party animal; we attacked each other; she is a hot chick; basic instinct. We degrade ourselves – and mainly the other – to an animal.

Or to a thing: "That's a good-looking 'thang'." "She" becomes "it".

In this situation, you're no longer talking about love. You're talking about lust. Lust uses the other person, abuses the other. Lust is purely egocentric and doesn't care about the feelings of the other. Lust releases hell on earth, as we have seen to the extreme in Rwanda.

The stimulation of the senses

Lust uses our senses. When Eve ate a fruit from the tree, that wasn't just a rational act. Eve saw the tree. She saw the apple shine. The fruit looked so beautiful. Maybe the tree even smelled great. She touched the fruit. She tasted it. She ate. Lust makes use of our senses. We see, smell, feel, taste. We eat.

What was so attractive about that woman? A hint of perfume? Her curves?

What is so beautiful about a new car? The smell of new leather? The sound of the engine?

A new pack of cigarettes? New clothes? New gadgets?

Senses.

Apple, with its expressive logo, knows exactly how this works, as do car manufacturers or coffee producers and winemakers. We allow ourselves to be guided by our senses. You probably have a closet full of (unworn?) clothes to prove it. Jesus also knows exactly how we work. When He talks about desiring a woman, He says:

> But I tell you that anyone who looks at a woman
> lustfully has already committed adultery with
> her in his heart. If your right eye causes you to
> stumble, gouge it out and throw it away. It is

*better for you to lose one part of your body than
for your whole body to be thrown into hell. And if
your right hand causes you to stumble, cut it off
and throw it away. It is better for you to lose one
part of your body than for your whole body to go
into hell. (Matthew 5:28–30)*

The intoxication of your thinking

Looking. Smelling. Fantasizing. Desiring. Lust literally means: "in your thinking". It has everything to do with the space that something occupies in your mind. You see a woman, and you want her. You think of her while you're busy working, while you're playing with your kids, talking with your customers. Your head is full of this woman, or the car, or the new computer. And the thing that you want slowly overtakes you. You become a slave. Lust is slavery.

The sentences of Jesus start so innocently. With looking. Desiring. But before you know it, He is talking about adultery. And hell. From just looking, straight to hell? How is that possible? Because, when we desire, we use the us–them, the me–it mindset. The princess becomes a beast. An object that serves for my pleasure or benefit. And afterwards? Oh, well.

Heaven is everywhere where God rules and where His beauty becomes visible. Hell is everywhere where people use each other and pursue their own needs based on Satan's deceit. And treat each other like animals. Or like a thing. The same powers that had their destructive effect in Rwanda are active within all of us.

Olaf

In Proverbs, Solomon focuses greatly on the topic of sexuality. A large portion of chapters 2 and 6 and all of chapters 5 and 7 are about the way a man must deal with woman, lust, and sexuality. In chapter 7, Solomon describes how a young man – let's call him Olaf – is walking down the street in the evening. Olaf is looking. His feet lead him to the squares and alleys that are known for the presence of willing women. In one of the squares, a woman approaches him. The tension rises. Solomon writes, "the night fell, the darkness spread." The pleasant-smelling woman with beautiful make-up who imposes herself on the young man is an unsatisfied woman. Her husband is often away from home. She feels lonely and says, "I left the house. I was looking for you." Isn't that the promise of an evening encounter? You are the one for me. You have what I am looking for. The woman seduces him with irresistible sentences that breathe sex:

> I have covered my bed with coloured linens from
> Egypt. I have perfumed my bed with myrrh, aloes
> and cinnamon. Come, let's drink deeply of love
> till morning; let's enjoy ourselves with love!

All of the young man's senses are stimulated. He sees, smells, feels, hears, and tastes. His entire mindset is possessed in anticipation of a night full of uninhibited sex. The young man joins her and has the night of his life.

He doesn't know that he died tonight.

> like an ox going to the slaughter, like a deer
> stepping into a noose till an arrow pierces his liver,

like a bird darting into a snare, little knowing it
will cost him his life. (Proverbs 7:22–23)

The slaughter of Olaf the Ox.

Solomon concludes his chapter as follows: "Her house is a highway to the grave, leading down to the chambers of death."

What seems like a night of shameless sex proves to be an entrance to the chambers of death. When you get enchanted by female beauty, you have taken a step towards hell. The woman has become an object. A vixen. Great for having fun, but then nothing.

Lust doesn't live up to its promise

In *The Three Musketeers*, d'Artagnan – although warned by his friends and, deep in his heart, aware of the fact that they are right – gets involved with Milady. D'Artagnan pretends to be someone else to win her affection. That is what lust does to us. We lose ourselves. Betray ourselves. We become someone else. Overcome with lust, d'Artagnan perseveres, only to discover that he has fallen hopelessly in love and that she didn't care about him at all. He thought he could use her, but instead she used him. She discards him. Even worse. She sends her murderous commandos to him and ultimately kills his childhood sweetheart.

That is what lust does to a man. It robs him of his dignity, his identity, and ultimately his life. Lust never lives up to its initial promises. Things are not as innocent as they seem. Sexuality is one of God's greatest inventions and yet at the same time so vulnerable that you must treat it with the greatest possible care.

How do we cope with lust?

Regarding how we cope with lust and temptation, we have good news and bad news. To start with, the bad news: it is an illusion to think that, once we are on this earth, temptation is a thing of the past. Temptation is a part of life. The good news is that you can actually lead a victorious life, without having to fall for temptations.

For starters, it is important to know what you want. Are you prepared to be radical? Do you want to live a pure life? Do you want to break with sin? As long as you are not sure about this, you are an easy prey for temptation. Olaf the Ox, from Proverbs 7, was wandering through the city. If the woman hadn't taken so much initiative, he wouldn't have ended up in her bed. He had a sort of "take it or leave it" attitude: "we'll see. I don't really want to, but you never know." It is good to express your radicalism. Towards God and friends. Jesus preaches radicalism: "When your eye or right hand (for most people their most dominant hand), seduces you to sin: be gone with it. Be radical."

In temptation, it is important to say no at the right time. Draw a line while you're still feeling strong. Don't seek out temptation, like Olaf, who consciously sauntered towards danger. We are beings who are easily influenced. There's a reason why there's a lot of money to be made in the advertising industry. If you know that certain people have a negative effect on you, or rob you of your sense of time, family, or dignity, don't associate with them. Avoid them. And conversely, surround yourself with people who inspire you and keep you sharp and help you live a pure life. Also be aware of the fact that there are moments when you are more vulnerable than normal. In America, support groups use the acronym HALT to this end. You are more vulnerable to temptation when you are **H**ungry, **A**ngry, **L**onely, or **T**ired. When you are in your HALT zone, make sure to build in extra safety.

Be open about your lust or struggle with a couple of reliable people. Bring matters into the light. It takes the sting of darkness out of your weakness. Your wife or your friends can pray for you, and after a while, ask you how you are doing in the field of sexuality. Some men wear a cross, or a special ring given to them by their wives. The jewellery reminds them of the covenant they made with God and their wife.

Since lust has everything to do with our mindset, it is important to focus our mindset on that which is "sacred, and pure, and good". For some men, it helps – in certain situations – to ask what Jesus would do. How would Jesus feel about what I am doing or thinking about right now? Contextualization is also a way to get your mind off the temptation of the moment. Thoughts such as "Yes, this is a beautiful woman, but maybe she is wearing dirty underwear" can have an extremely sobering effect. Or imagine what you'll lose (in terms of boldness, freedom, joy, and confidence) if you give in to temptation.

Offensive prayer

A method that has helped me (Henk) in my battle against lust is offensive prayer. When a temptingly beautiful woman enters my mind, I have an option. Will I give in to temptation? Or will I do something else with it? Martin Luther said, "You can't keep the birds from flying over your head, but you can prevent them from building a nest in your hair." I have learned to use the flight of the bird as a reason to pray for my relationship (including sexual relationship) with my wife, Ruth. My reasoning was "Every time the devil wants to tackle me by using a temptation, I use the temptation as a trigger to ask for extra blessing of my relationship with Ruth. This way, the temptation of the devil backfires. The more he tempts me, the more I pray for my wife and for our relationship, and the better it becomes. At some point, he will grow tired and try something else." This strategy has had a wonderful effect for me, in every sense.

Wherever Solomon writes about lust, temptation, or sexuality, he says very little about the proper way to do it. He – justly – gives abundant warnings. But he doesn't provide any tips and tricks. It's as if he wants to say, "I'll leave that to your creativity and playfulness."

Love or lust

In the journey of the boy with the hessian sack to the man on a mission, the proper way to deal with love and lust is essential. Pursuing your lust robs you of your male strength, boldness, and confidence. Leave lust behind you.

Sexuality is about so much more than the physical act of sex between man and woman. Sexuality – in the deepest sense of the word – is about the life energy given by God, which is reflected in a true coexistence.

Intimacy.

Love.

Use your sexual energy to give beauty, dignity, and life to those who have to do without.

13

Ting

The three friends – for, as we have said, Athos had sworn not to stir a foot to equip himself – went out early in the morning, and returned late at night. They wandered about the streets, looking at the pavement as if to see whether the passengers had not left a purse behind them. They might have been supposed to be following tracks, so observant were they wherever they went. When they met they looked desolately at one another, as much as to say, "Have you found anything?"

ALEXANDRE DUMAS

Someone once asked me what I (Henk) would be preaching about on the coming Sunday. "About giving," I replied. "Oh, I'll stay home then," he responded. The only book I have written that I know was torn to pieces was about money. Apparently, the topic of money generates intense emotions. In various churches, we see how the management is struggling to properly shape the important theme of "giving". Giving is a sensitive matter. Especially when you have been almost broke yourself. Still, it is a topic that can't be skipped in a men's book. After all, most men deal with money regularly. Jesus Himself frequently talked about money as well. In the chapter on the theological significance of the ostrich, we talked about Jesus' joke of the camel and the needle. That was humour indeed, but His joke had a radical twist:

> .... it is easier for a camel to go through the eye
> of a needle than for someone who is rich to enter
> the kingdom of God. (Matthew 19:24)

People who laughed about the image of the camel and the needle didn't think it was so funny when they thought about what it meant. It is easier for a camel to crawl through the eye of a needle than for someone who makes £100,000 per year to enter the kingdom of God. Imagine the nervous shuffling of feet, the avoidance of eye contact, the shock, the annoyance. Jesus always does that! Everybody is having great fun, and then He throws in a one-liner that makes you shiver.

In reply, the disciples stammer: "Who then can be saved?" (Matthew 19:25)

Apparently, money stands in the way of our salvation before you know it. Being good with money is essential, apparently. But what does "being good with money" mean, according to Jesus?

Two extremes

In the history of Christianity, the perspective on this has always fluctuated between two extremes. On the one hand, there were people like Francis of Assisi, who took the commandment of Jesus to sell everything and give everything away very literally. Wear a hairy robe, tie a rope around it, and follow Jesus into the wide world. Don't take any money, or a travel bag, or a second set of clothes. Nothing. That is one extreme. This radical following of Jesus is powered by a range of statements by Jesus, in the context of "Do not store up for yourselves treasures on earth" (Matthew 6:19) and "go, sell your possessions and give to the poor, and you will have treasure in heaven. Then come, follow me" (Matthew 19:21). That's all very clear. However, it's not the whole story.

The other extreme is inspired by men such as Luther and Calvin. Their slogan was work hard, make a lot of money, save a lot, and give a lot away. This work ethic forms the theological foundation of the American Dream. And this lifestyle can also cite a lot of Bible passages in its defence: the rich Roman centurion Cornelius is one of the few people in the Gospels who is applauded for his great faith. Apparently, religion and wealth can go hand in hand after all. Jesus Himself was supported by a group of rich women who followed Him. The good Samaritan was not a pauper. He had enough money to make a down payment for the inn before he had to continue on his trade mission. Both poverty and wealth can be defended from a biblical perspective. So the question remains: How should we deal with money?

Jesus' strangest parable

In Luke 16, Jesus tells what is, perhaps, His strangest parable. For centuries, Bible interpreters have been having difficulty interpreting this story. It is as follows: A landowner lived in a beautiful villa in the big city. From time to time, he visited his estates in the countryside. He didn't like what he saw during one of his visits. He had entrusted one of his farms to a manager, but this manager made a mess of things. The landowner fired his manager on the spot. He was given one last assignment: Draw up the final statement. The manager was upset. What should he do? He said to himself, "I am a lousy digger, and I'm too ashamed to become a beggar. What should I do?"

Ting!

Then, the manager had an idea. He told all the debtors of his boss he spoke to that week that they could eliminate a part of their debt. This would give him a couple of addresses where he could stay when he had no place to live next week.

Up until this point, it is just a normal story. There is a bad guy. He steals from his boss. What has to happen to the bad guy? How does God respond to so much dishonesty? Verses 8–9 state:

> *And the master was furious with the dishonest*
> *land agent and exclaimed: "What?" You dishonest*
> *land agent! First I fire you on the spot because*
> *of your dishonesty, and then you rob me of even*
> *more money? And Jesus said: "Don't be dishonest*
> *and steal no money, but be a reliable employee*
> *and do what's good."*

Is this what it says?

Not really. Although you might expect something of that sort. But in reality, Jesus said:

> *The master commended the dishonest manager*
> *because he had acted shrewdly. For the people*
> *of this world are more shrewd in dealing with*
> *their own kind than are the people of the light.*
> *I tell you, use worldly wealth to gain friends for*

yourselves, so that when it is gone, you will be
welcomed into eternal dwellings.

The master praised the dishonest land manager.

Jesus invites us to follow the example of the impostor and to use money in such a way that it paves the road to heaven for us. Money can't just keep you from entering heaven; it can also get you in. But how? "Use the dishonest land manager as an example," Jesus says. Excuse me? Does Jesus ask us to steal from our bosses, to forge invoices, and to eliminate the debt of others?

The lesson is a little more subtle.

Jesus says: "Look at that dishonest manager. Because the world is often more shrewd than Christians when it comes to money, make friends with the help of the false mammon, so that, when you enter heaven and money plays no role whatsoever any more, you will have friends to turn to." Use your money in such a way that you have friends when money no longer exists.

Money isn't neutral

It is striking to see how Jesus refers to money. He isn't just talking about money. He is talking about the foul mammon.

The.

Foul.

Mammon.

These three words expose the nature of the power behind the money. Jesus presents money as a personal power: the mammon. He presents money as a god: Mammon. And he shows us the true nature of this personal power: foul. It literally says: *a-dikos*. Not good. Evil. One possible way to render this would be: "Make your friends with the help of the money devil."

Use the money devil in such a way that it benefits your salvation. Use what is bad to do something good. It sounds shrewd, don't you think? About as shrewd as the dishonest land agent.

By introducing the idea of the foul mammon, Jesus wants to show us that money is more than a collection of coins and bills. Money isn't neutral.

People in the world are often more aware of this than Christians. Money is more than the sum of the parts. Fifty pounds is more than fifty pounds. A million isn't just a million. A million can be worth a human life, or ten. A million can be worth a marriage, or a relationship with your children. How many men have sacrificed their families on the altar of money? Always working, missing out on your children's childhood, so that you can make £30,000 more on an annual basis. Thirty thousand pounds – or your children!

People have been killed over their Nikes or over other clothing. People compromise their integrity for money. People sometimes ignore each other for years over money. We give money a power that belongs only to God: money makes people happy; money protects; money earns you status, respect, power, well-being. People lie, steal, cheat, become grumpy, or worry about money. We fight wars over oil. Money.

Money isn't neutral. People compromise their health or integrity for a little money.

There was once a contest in America: "What is the craziest thing you'd do for $10,000 in cash?" The winner was a man who ate a ten-foot-tall tree, from the top to the roots, including leaves, bark, and trunk. It took him 18 hours. Then he had a stomach ache.

That is America, but we're no different in the Netherlands. Terror Jaap was a participant in the television show *The Golden Cage*. The finalists had to vote for each other, for who they thought should win the grand prize. Jaap said, "I will give half of the money to my favourite charity." He won the prize, and then said, in front of all the viewers in the Netherlands, "My favourite charity is me."

As soon as silver enters the stage

Money is a sensitive subject. A study into the biggest taboo in the relationship between a therapist and a patient resulted in – money. For a counsellor, it would be wiser to sleep with your client than to lend them money.

Apart from the kingdom of God, there wasn't a topic that was addressed more often by Jesus than money. Why? Because our interaction with money says a lot about who we are. Money is a god. It gets under your skin. It overtakes you. That is how we talk about ourselves and others: "He is rich." Or "He is poor." These are identity statements.

A rich, old, unhappy man once asked a wise rabbi for advice. "I am so unhappy," the old curmudgeon complained. The rabbi replied, "Look out of the windows. What do you see?" "I see all kinds of people," the man replied. "Now look in the mirror," the rabbi asked, "and tell me what you see." "I see myself," the man said. The rabbi looked at the old man and said, "The window is made of glass. The mirror is as well, but the mirror comes with a thin layer of silver. And as soon as silver enters the stage, we tend to lose sight of all other people and only see ourselves."

Sly as a fox

How should we deal with the foul mammon?

Be as cunning as the dishonest land agent, and do what the money devil doesn't expect. Jesus Himself was cunning enough to lure Satan into his own trap. Ever since Jesus set foot on earth, Satan had been trying to kill Jesus. Every single time, the attempts to murder the Son of God failed. Until the devil finally found a way. Judas was prepared to betray Him. The Pharisees were so angry that they were willing to kill Him. Pilate was so weak that he was willing to succumb. And Jesus allowed everything to happen. I can imagine Satan was holding his sulphurous breath when Jesus was nailed to the cross. Would his arch enemy have one final trick up His – proverbial – sleeve? But nothing happened. Jesus allowed Himself to be killed. He gave up His spirit.

Satan rejoiced. The realm of the dead was shaking because of the shrieking of countless of demons. Finally, they had won. The Son of God was dead! Their plan had worked.

However, for Satan, the cross would prove to be a place of defeat, not of victory. At Golgotha, Lucifer dug his own grave. He made soldiers scourge Jesus to death, and he didn't notice that his own skull was being crushed. How cunning the cross was. Jesus misled Satan and beat him with his own weapons, because a brain as small as that of the devil can't understand that someone would give his life for the evil of others.

Along the same lines: Treat the money devil the way it doesn't expect you to.

Give it away.

There is only room for one thought in the small brain of the foul mammon: "People want to have, have, have me. More and more. People are willing to steal, lie, and deceive for me.

Even kill for me. Nobody can resist my attractive force."

And then, all of a sudden, there are people who give him away like it's nothing. There you go, £100 to charity. The money devil can't understand that. But this is the way to use money to make friends for all eternity. Be as sly as a fox and treat money in the most profane, heartless way you can think of, and give.

God doesn't need your money, but you need giving

Since giving is so opposite to the nature of money, it is the most effective way to be released from the power of the mammon. Jesus said, "Look at the cunningness of the bad manager. Do what the master doesn't expect." Every time you give away money, you give yourself a little more freedom, and you give yourself the opportunity to trust in God some more, instead of trusting in money. God doesn't need your money. You need giving.

"Gather treasures in heaven," Jesus told the people. "Because where your treasure is, that is where your heart will be." Your heart follows your treasure. You can consider your life to be your final destination. All wealth and resources that you gather, you keep to yourself. You buy luxuries and invest in opportunities for more wealth. Eventually, you're on top of a mountain of treasures, all for you.

You can also see your life as the process of moving. You load all of your treasures into a big moving truck, destination heaven. You follow it in your passenger car, only carrying what you really need. Everything you were able to send ahead, you loaded into the truck, destination heaven. When your passenger car reaches its destination, you'll be able to experience what blessing your treasures were able to spread. You will meet friends you didn't even know existed:

a small boy in India who was able to go to school because you invested in his church; a grateful mother who embraces you because you bought food for her children; a man who – because of your microloan – was able to start his own business and who is now able to take care of his family again. Handle the money entrusted to you by God wisely, so that you have friends when money no longer plays a role. Paul writes to Timothy:

> *Command those who are rich in this present world not to be arrogant nor to put their hope in wealth, which is so uncertain, but to put their hope in God, who richly provides us with everything for our enjoyment. Command them to do good, to be rich in good deeds, and to be generous and willing to share. In this way they will lay up treasure for themselves as a firm foundation for the coming age, so that they may take hold of the life that is truly life. (1 Timothy 6:17–19)*

Every man can choose between a lifestyle that is characterized by giving or one that is characterized by taking. Men who learn to be generous will notice that their hessian sack will be significantly lighter. There is less reason for worry. You'll have more friends, and the smothering effect of the money devil loses its grip on your soul. It is not just about you. It is about all the people to whom you can be a blessing, because of your life. God doesn't entrust you with thousands of pounds so that you can take care of yourself and no one else. Your abundance means that you have a responsibility for people who have less.

14

Fleeing towards the sun

*D'Artagnan concealed his face in the bosom of
Athos, and sobbed aloud.*

*"Weep," said Athos, "weep, heart full of love,
youth, and life! Alas, would I could weep like
you!"*

*And he drew away his friend, as affectionate as
a father, as consoling as a priest, noble as a man
who has suffered much.*

ALEXANDRE DUMAS

The news hit me (Theo) like a sledgehammer – about what
happened in Afghanistan to a boy only 13 years old. Still
a child, supposed to play soccer with his friends on a field
near home, not a care in the world, he was tortured by 200
Taliban warriors. How that happened and how long it took,
they didn't say. Afterwards, he was shot to death. I don't
want to try and imagine how that must have happened.
But the heartbreaking photo of that one tree on that bare
field, where they hung the lifeless boy before the eyes of
the community, is imprinted in my memory. The reason for
this atrocity was that the boy had assisted the Americans on
their base a few miles ahead. With what? That wasn't clear.

Frozen

This is not about me making a reasoned judgment about who the good guys and the bad guys are here. This is about something else. This is about that news item and that photo. That photo symbolizes everything that loss does. Loss freezes. It changes life from a movie into a frozen image. The world keeps spinning, but not in the village of that boy. There, the movie has been frozen. And while the world continues to move ahead, that small Afghan community that was once so peaceful is stuck in that single moment. Staring. They are the eyes of those who intensely loved that boy.

They. See. A. Lifeless. Boy. Hanging. From. A. Tree.

And nobody is aware yet of the dark times that are ahead. Of what this significant loss really means.

Astounding, isn't it? At the end of a long day at work, I turn on the television. I look at the powerful photograph. It affects me greatly. And I turn off the television and help my wife to set the table. My life goes on. But still, as I am serving dinner, the movie of life has frozen again, and again, and again, at countless places in the world, and probably even in my own street.

Loss breaks in

If life is a movie, then loss turns it into a frozen image. And while the entire world moves on, your life is frozen. That is how loss always works. It breaks in. It introduces an unexpected end to the past (as it was), to the future (as you hoped it would be), and to the present (as you live it). You don't just have to say goodbye to how it was, but also to how it could have been. Your mother calls to tell you that your father has suddenly died. What was never said will remain unsaid. Your wife comes home to pack her things. She is moving out. Permanently. The doctor has to inform you that your disease is incurable. The bed becomes a prison. What was supposed to be finished will never be finished. Your newborn has a disability. Your employer has no choice and has to cut the workforce. Your older brother tells you about abuse in the family. After a long journey together, you find out that you're infertile. You did everything you could, but you can't prevent one of your children from being evicted from his or her home. You were optimistic, but after three years, the company still went bankrupt.

Two little shoes that would never be worn

When I was a teenager, the phone rang. I answered: "Hi, this is Theo." The female voice sounded rushed: "Is your father home?" I didn't think so, otherwise he would have answered the phone, so I replied: "No, he's not here." "Oh," the woman replied, after which she said, "Could you please tell your father that I found my husband, dead in his chair?" "Eh, I will," was the only thing that I could say in shock. And that was it. I remember that I knew who her husband was. I couldn't stop my thoughts from imagining the scene.

One of my childhood friends got married. He and his wife were a beautiful couple. But within a year, it was all over. They lost what they once had, or they never achieved what they had desired so much.

Harmke (my wife) and I had built a beautiful friendship with Vicken and Salpi in Athens, back when we lived in Greece. Salpi was a wonderful cook, so we celebrated our friendship with the most delicious meals. Two years later,

Vicken had to inform us of the fact that, after a coma of 45 days, Salpi had died. She had left him with two young children. The last time I talked to him, the grief was almost too much to bear.

Earlier this year, an Egyptian friend spent a couple of days at our place. Jokes about Dutch cuisine and fun with snow, something he had never seen before, alternated with deep conversations about life. His eight-month-old daughter had been suffering from cancer for half of her life. But the baby was expected to recover. So, before he left, we put two little shoes in his suitcase. Shortly thereafter, we received word that the little girl had lost her battle against the disease.

Loss can't be measured

Some people have the questionable ability to compare loss and grief. But loss is loss. It can't be measured. All losses are painful, each in its own way. Which of the people in the above-mentioned examples has suffered the greatest loss? This simply isn't the right question.

Every loss is unique and causes unique pain. Comparison only leads to unhealthy extremes. At one extreme, people with a "greater" loss may think that nobody has ever suffered as much as they have, meaning that nobody will understand and that nobody can help them. The inevitable result of this attitude is that they drown in a swamp of self-pity. At the other extreme, people with a "smaller" loss suddenly lose their right to be sad, because, how bad is it, really? It's not that terrible, right? As if you can only mourn when your arm is amputated, but you have to suck it up when your arm is only broken!

So, it is not about the question of which loss is worse. But what is it about? The crucial question is: How do you respond to substantial loss?

Winning or losing

Loss is inevitable. Sooner or later, everybody faces it, some more than others, sometimes hidden, sometimes visible. When it concerns confrontation with loss, the world doesn't consist of winners and losers, but only losers. However, we can win or lose in the way that we respond to the loss and in the way that we deal with the pain.

Author and religious philosopher Jerry Sitsser lost his mother, his wife Lynda, and his daughter Diana Jane in one tragic car crash. He survived the accident, together with his daughter Catherine and his sons David and John. In his touching and brutally honest book *A Grace Disguised*, he describes a dream he had after a terrifying moment of deep darkness:

I dreamed of a setting sun. I was frantically running west, trying desperately to catch it and remain in its fiery warmth and light. But, I was losing the race. The sun was beating me to the horizon and was soon gone. I suddenly found myself in the twilight. Exhausted, I stopped running and glanced with foreboding over my shoulder to the east. I saw a vast darkness closing in on me. I was terrified by that darkness. I wanted to keep running after the sun, though I knew that it was futile, for it had already proven itself faster than I was. So I lost all hope, collapsed to the ground, and fell into despair.

*I thought at that moment that I would live in
darkness forever. I felt absolute terror in my soul.*

Fleeing towards the sun or running through the darkness

There are two ways to respond to loss: by running westwards
or by turning eastwards. You can run for the loss or decide
to face it. You can deny the pain or continue living. Running
westwards seems more appealing. It means fleeing towards
the setting sun. Running eastwards requires more courage.
It is the route straight through darkness. But it is also the
fastest route to the sun and the light of the day. The choice
between east and west is essential. Sitsser says about this:

*We make it unnecessarily worse when we allow
our loss to lead to more loss: the gradual demise
of our soul, our heart.*

And a couple of pages later:

*A poor choice will make our heart die, and that
death is worse than that of a loved one, or the
loss of your job or your health.*

We men do not tend to turn eastwards. We are not very
fond of facing our feelings.

Why is that?

Manu Keirse, author of popular books about loss and
sadness, says:

Starting in their childhood, men are continually encouraged to refrain from expressing their emotions. "Big boys don't cry, right?" Instead of discussing emotions or showing them, men tend to vent them through work and activity. They have to be strong and are encouraged to take on a protective and active role. Often, it is difficult for them to be close to others in their emotions or to provide adequate support. They tend to stay far away from everything related to emotions.

And also:

The relationships of men are often more focused on activities than on emotions. They tend to be more competitive, and weakness is often not permitted. In moments of sadness, they have fewer people that they can rely on and less experience in expressing and sharing emotions.

Men are "strong". Men are doers. Men do not cry. Men keep on going. And so on. Men get lonely. Men get isolated. Men wonder: Where did it go wrong? Where did I lose my heart? Where did my energy, strength, and vitality go? Why can't I embrace life as I once did? Why am I starting to doubt whether I ever embraced life?

Embarrassment

We frequently encounter men who are ashamed of their feelings of grief and pain, whose shame comes from a sense of "not doing it right". Because if "you're strong" and "have your feelings in check", then "you're doing it right". A "balanced man" shall be "rational" at any given time. At least, that is the general belief. I (Theo) once met a man who had lost his sister almost ten years ago. At home, they didn't talk about it. Life went on. Now, he is stuck. Things aren't going well at work. He is completely stuck. Loss can't be suppressed. Fleeing towards the sun doesn't work. The sun sets faster than you can run.

I also talked to a man who had lost his father recently. I asked him whether he could find a way through the loss and the grief. He replied: "Yes, I'm doing fine, but it takes longer than I had anticipated." I decided to ask how long ago he had lost his father. His answer is as surprising as it is revealing: "Six weeks."

Curious, I asked him what he had expected. Your father dies. When that happens, something inside you dies. You shouldn't try to avoid this grief. You can admit that you are too restless to sit on the couch, too apathetic to do anything. You can say that you are annoyed by people who – with good intentions – try to comfort you by saying that your father is Home. "Yes," you think, "that's right, but I'm still here and I miss him." You can communicate that you're not doing OK, that you have trouble praying, that you are angry and confused, that feelings of despair and bitterness overwhelm you, that there was too much pain in the relationship, which will now be much harder to heal. It will, and should, last a while, before you can give that grief a place in your heart. And generally, that time is more than six weeks.

"You never cry, do you?"

A couple of weeks ago, my son Manuel (four years old) said out of the blue: "Hey, Dad?" "Yes?" "You never cry, do you?" I was perplexed. There's frequently more going on in his head than I suspect. And it also startled me. I suddenly realized, more than I had before, that Manuel is already looking at his father. By looking at me, he is trying to understand how life works. As a father, I have a huge impact on the emotional development of my sons and daughter. Gordon MacDonald underlines this with a painful example:

> Do you remember being a child, and something would happen that was extremely disappointing to you? You could hardly hold in your tears. So there you are, trying to get yourself together, trying not to cry. But it doesn't work, and you start crying. And your father yells: "Stop crying. Or I'll give you something to cry about. You're such a crybaby!" I still hear those words – "you are such a crybaby!" – every time I feel an emotion developing.

"Do you want to know how serious it is? Can you handle it?"

By the way, it isn't true that I never cry. Although I had suffered my share of losses before, brokenness entered my life three years ago, at full speed, and more intensely than ever. It was April 2007, when my sister – who is three years older – was diagnosed with cancer. She had been working as an oncology nurse. After consulting with her department head about complaints she had, they decided to run some scans. It didn't look good. They immediately proceeded to further examination. I remember exactly when the seriousness of the situation hit me. I was in Beijing, and

I called my sister to congratulate her on her birthday. She was in hospital at that point. She told me that she was going to be operated on in two days, and that there was a lot of concern about the outcome of the operation. She asked me: "Do you want to know how bad it is? Can you handle that?" I didn't know if I could, but I said: "Yes." She told me that she was taking into account the fact that her lifespan on earth might be very limited. Never before had I been confronted with a possible loss by a death so close to me. I was shocked. In the months that followed, her health deteriorated rapidly. The chemotherapy had no effect. They were months, weeks, and days of fewer and fewer options. Not only my sister, but our entire family, was exposed to a roller coaster of emotions and thoughts. It was an exhausting time. There were too many contradictions. Time had frozen, but life went on. It felt surreal, but it was really happening. It was really happening, but we couldn't understand it. Sometimes we understood, but then we wished that it wasn't happening. And eventually… it goes so quickly, but it takes so long. We don't want to miss you, but please, sweetheart, let go. But despite the struggle with her illness, there was the peace of God. And despite the thousands of questions without answers, there was deep peace in Jesus. After five months of illness, my sister died of cancer. She was 31 years old. The first thing I felt was relief. No more suffering. A couple of hours later, the first tears emerged. Suddenly I became aware of it: never again. They were the most intense tears I had ever cried.

How do you respond?

At some point in the months after the loss, you have to make a choice: How will I respond? It is the ultimate choice every man faces when loss attacks him, loss in any form, big or small, hidden or visible, sooner or later. It is the choice between denial or continuing to live. Between the path of the boy or the path of the man.

Imagine that we choose the eastward run into the darkness, the path of facing the pain wherever possible, the hardest but quickest path to the light. What would that run look like?

Curve ten

A father lost his son to cancer when he was just ten years old. The man, a cyclist, climbed a mountain in the French Alps six times in one day, in the context of a charity promotion for the fight against cancer. And every time, curve ten was the hardest. Because every time, he would think of his son.

Dealing with a loss is like climbing a mountain. The road ahead is steep, difficult, and tough. There are moments when you feel as if you can hardly go on. But you still do. You would rather flee, but you know that the right path is the path forward. Persevere. There are moments when everything hurts... all of your body, all of your emotions. Sometimes, you want to give in to your mood. And sometimes, you try to drown yourself out. You simply say that you're doing fine and couldn't be doing any better. There are moments when you would like nothing more than to bury yourself in an abundance of harmful and unhealthy things, simply to forget everything. Sometimes you think that it might help to fool yourself: "I am not climbing a steep mountain. This is simply a flat country road." But you know it won't help. You have to persevere. There is just one way to overcome the loss. And that is by continuing to live.

A more beautiful person

Climbing the mountain is not a one-off event. You'll have to go up several times, live through your grief again and again. And just when you thought you had left this chapter in your life behind you, it still comes back. Like the father who felt the grief more intensely in curve number ten. But along the way, you'll notice that the grief will become less sharp. Along the way, you'll notice that you'll be able to enjoy normal things again. You'll discover that you have changed. Side issues have become less critical, and you have a better grasp of what is truly important. With each hairpin curve that you conquer, you discover that you have a desire to spend more time with the people you love. You show more appreciation for friends. You let go of expectations of people and start to think more about how God feels about you. You start to focus more on the here and now. You sense that loss also has a cathartic effect. You become a more beautiful person.

You discover that the Heavenly Father has turned it in your favour by turning you into more of a man.

Climb the mountain, identify the loss, and live through the pain. Turn eastwards. Through the darkness.

15

I forgive you

"And I," said d'Artagnan,… "I forgive you and cry over you."

ALEXANDRE DUMAS

Nobody gets through their childhood, youth, and the rest of their life unscathed. People get hurt and hurt others. We get injured, and we injure others. The Australian psychologist Julie Fitness studied which things people in intimate relationships struggled to forgive each other for. She discovered that people would have a hard time forgiving their spouse if they commit adultery or hurt their children. Fathers find it hard to forgive their daughter for sleeping around. Parents have a hard time forgiving their son when he breaks the law.

Hurtful actions of others, but also sentences of — for instance — rejection (nobody can love you), perfectionism (why didn't you finish in first place?), or negative prediction (you'll never amount to anything) can sting and have long-term repercussions. Equally painful is the fact that the deepest wounds are often inflicted by the people who can hit you the hardest. American theologian Neil Anderson says about this:

Of the hundreds of people that I have counseled, ninety five percent put their father or mother at the top of the list. Three of the first four names are often immediate family.

Joseph, the man who was hit

Someone who was hit the hardest by the people closest to him was Joseph. His brothers couldn't stand him due to his self-confidence, the fact that he was his father's favourite, and also because of the strange dreams that he had. In those dreams, everything was about Joseph, and they had to bow to him. The feelings that Joseph's brothers had towards him started to escalate. First, they intensely disliked him and they couldn't spare a kind word for him. Then, they started to hate him. Finally, they felt like killing him. And they almost did. But eventually, his brothers chose instead to sell him as a slave to Egypt. The attempted murder and selling him as a slave were both intense forms of betrayal of their own brother. With that, the brothers inflicted deep wounds on Joseph's soul. Once in Egypt, he did well as a slave in the house of Potiphar. But when Potiphar's wife falsely accused Joseph of assaulting her, he was sent to prison. Once again, hurt. In prison, Joseph was soon given managerial tasks, because the prison guard was very satisfied with him. Via the interpretation of a number of dreams, Joseph found his way to the court of the Pharaoh, the highest ruler in the country.

And then came the moment when Joseph had to face the confrontation with his past. His brothers had come to Egypt to buy grain, due to a severe famine in the land of Canaan. They were standing in front of Joseph, but they didn't realize it. Joseph did. And he knew who he was.

He was no longer the younger 17-year-old brother in the beautiful coat who they could throw into a well or get rid of by tying him to a caravan. He was an adult and the powerful viceroy of Egypt.

What will he do?

It would have been easy for Joseph to take revenge on his brothers, to take matters into his own hands. His brothers had first thrown him into the well, then condemned him to slavery, and later made him end up in prison. All because of his brothers. In an instant, he could have made his brothers pay for their stupidities. Joseph had an option: Shall I forgive my brothers or not? Shall I let go of my hateful feelings towards the people who have hurt me? Shall I let go of my right to revenge and retribution? Shall I leave this to God?

What did Joseph do?

> Then Joseph could no longer control himself before all his attendants, and he cried out, "Have everyone leave my presence!" So there was no one with Joseph when he made himself known to his brothers. And he wept so loudly that the Egyptians heard him, and Pharaoh's household heard about it. Joseph said to his brothers, "I am Joseph! Is my father still living?" But his brothers were not able to answer him, because they were terrified at his presence. (Genesis 45:1–3)

Joseph forgave. He let God rule. The five words say it all: "Is my father still alive?"

And the brothers? They were shocked, and they were still afraid that Joseph would take his revenge once their father, Jacob, had died. But Joseph had truly forgiven them. He comforted them:

> *"Don't be afraid. Am I in the place of God? You intended to harm me, but God intended it for good to accomplish what is now being done, the saving of many lives. So then, don't be afraid. I will provide for you and your children." And he reassured them and spoke kindly to them. (Genesis 50:19–21)*

Forgiving is sometimes terrible, and sometimes seems impossible

Joseph forgave. He was even able to comfort and reassure them. But before he did so, he struggled. First, he tested his brothers and took his time. Forgiving is often a difficult process. Having to forgive is sometimes terrible and often seems impossible. We can feel so betrayed, abandoned, or hurt that forgiving is the last thing on our mind. And the last thing we are willing to do. Anger, frustration, and indignation for the injustice done to us together form a mixture of (intense) emotions in our heart. Those emotions have a right to exist. They show us that we believe that there is a higher moral code, that we look for justice, and that we believe that hurting people, injustice, and evil are not OK. Sometimes, these emotions involve thoughts such as: "I'll make him pay for this. From now on, I'll keep my distance. I would like something bad to happen to him." It is in our nature to want the person who hurt us to feel just as much pain as we did.

Positively nauseating

I (Theo) was talking to a father who had to forgive his son-in-law (Johan). He said:

My daughter (Janneke) is currently going through a divorce. Johan cheated on her in a terrible way. He played in a band, was often out very late, got drunk, and would mingle with women. One night, he took two women home. How humiliating do you think this was for Janneke? In addition, he abused her and he took no responsibility whatsoever for their two-year-old son. He has yet to change a single diaper, and he never picks up the kid to build a connection. You know what he says? "Oh well, he doesn't notice anything. He is way too young for that. Later, when he's older, I'll just tell him that I love him."

It wasn't until the marriage was about to burst that my daughter came to me. I asked her why she didn't come to me sooner, so that I could have helped her. She was ashamed. She did everything she could to save her marriage. Every day, she made him breakfast in bed, just to keep showing love from her side. She did it every single day. Until her husband's employer called her: "I caught Johan in bed with my wife. Red-handed."

Her disgust was so intense that she literally had to throw up. Then, enough was enough. Janneke is currently living with us again.

I asked him whether he had forgiven Johan. He replied, "Yes, I was furious. But eventually, I was able to forgive him." I admire him.

How does the process of forgiveness work?

Forgiving is not the same as pretending that what happened to you isn't bad. Nor does it mean that the pain is gone instantly. Forgiving is not a synonym for forgetting. In addition, forgiving doesn't mean that the relationship will be exactly as it used to be. Forgiving means that you free yourself from the other who has wounded you. When Peter asks Jesus, "How often should I forgive? Seven times?" Jesus replies, "Not seven times, I tell you, but seventy times seven." That is a very deliberate statement by Jesus, because you often have to forgive someone countless times for the same thing. Not because the other does the same to you 490 times, but because it is stuck in your head 490 times. That painful scene in your mind endlessly repeats itself. Forgiving means taking the DVD of that moment out of the player and storing it on the shelf. If you don't do that, it works like a slow and powerful poison that further damages your insides. Forgiving means saying, "I will no longer allow my life to be controlled by what you did to me. You cost me enough energy as it is. You have stolen enough years from me. I forgive you." That doesn't always have to be done in a kind way. A woman who was abused by her grandfather, said: "I have forgiven him, the b____!"

Sometimes, that's the only way to do it. "I forgive you, you b____!" It is good to express forgiveness out loud. Often, that has an extremely liberating effect. It is also powerful and healing to do it in the presence of others, for instance, together with brothers at church or good friends.

They can support you, pray for you, and are witnesses of your decision to forgive. Subsequently, they can help you to move on with your life.

Are there people in your environment that you still have to forgive because of what they did to you recently or long ago? Are there any painful scenes that are consistently present in your mind? These may be deep and big wounds. But they can also be relatively small wounds, of which we are sometimes not even aware, but that eat at us anyway. It brings relief if we also clean up those "smaller things" through forgiveness. This is something that I (Theo) have experienced in person.

In a small village

I grew up in a village in Zeeland. The village was small and safe. The school was within walking distance, and all my friends lived nearby. Of course, we all had BMX bicycles, and we knew how to ride them. I frequently came home covered in mud, from my back to my hair. My mother was often very worried when she saw me through the window, racing between the apple trees in the orchard. I remember that on the day that my little brother was born, I had crashed with my bike, big time, not in the orchard, but on an undeveloped piece of land. I was racing through the mud at high speed when my front wheel hit a pit in the ground, and I made a very unsuccessful somersault. I will never forget that day, not because I fell, but because my little brother was born.

I had a wonderful childhood in that small village, except for one thing: my neighbour. He disliked me, and I disliked him. But he was older and stronger. He and his friends would ride their bicycles across town, looking for their prey. And when I was playing in the street with my friends, "those big boys" would sometimes – under the supervision of my neighbour – surround me with their bicycles. "Got a problem?" they would ask, and that really intimidated me. And humiliated me too. As soon as one of my friends or I saw a hole in the cordon of bicycles, we would make a run for the nearest safe backyard. We had escaped unscathed yet again.

I also remembered another event. Our neighbours had built a big pool in the backyard and they invited me to come over and swim. I loved that. From my roof window, I had been looking at the blue water, desiring to be in it, And now I had the opportunity to do just that. So I decided to take them up on their offer. It was fun, but not for long. It ended with my neighbour bullying me.

And I can also vividly remember another situation. One day, we were playing hide-and-seek with a group of kids on our street. Hide-and-seek meant excitement and adventure. You would feel your heart pound. We had just finished playing hide-and-seek when my neighbour walked up to us. He was carrying something in his hands, and it was on. It was a gas burner. And the flame was huge. He chased me with it. As a kid, that leaves you with three options: punch hard, run hard, or both. I chose the second, because running was what I did best. It was just one of his jokes... of course. Very funny! As a kid, I clearly had a very different sense of humour than he did.

Due to all of this bullying, I hated my neighbour.

When I was ten years old, we moved. I went to a new school, made new friends, and entered a new phase. I didn't think about my childhood much. Years later, I had to be somewhere in Zeeland, and I often drove past the small village where I grew up. I was together with my wife, and I wanted to show her where I had lived as a child. So we drove to the village. In reality, everything was much smaller than I remembered. Back then – as a child – you had to walk all the way down the street, then turn left, and walk all the way down another street to reach the school. I remember thinking it was a long walk. Now, through the eyes of an adult, the street wasn't as long and wide as I remembered.

And as I walked there, I felt it.

It was there. Unnoticed and quietly, it had kept itself hidden. Like a fire that smoulders in your stomach. And it flared in the form of a sudden sense of anger. Because I was back there. The village. The street. The house. The neighbour. And what I would have wanted to do so badly back then, but was afraid to, now emerged in my mind as an angry line: If I run into him now, I will beat him to pulp.

Suddenly, I realized that the bullying of my neighbour had affected me more than I had thought. These emotions had been dormant deep inside of me, and I had forgotten about them. But now, they suddenly awoke. I felt anger and outrage. And I realized that I had to forgive my neighbour, because I hadn't done so yet. And I really wanted to forgive, because I didn't want to keep carrying around "potatoes" of lack of forgiveness – not even small ones – in my hessian sack on my journey to the top of the mountain. I refuse to allow anger to simmer somewhere, hidden beneath the surface of my soul. I want my heart to breathe and grow in its ability to give and receive love.

Christmas dinner

Whether it concerns big or small things, forgiveness is essential. Nobody wants to have awkward situations about where people should sit at Christmas dinner. Nobody wants to "not be in touch" with their parents, brothers, or sisters. Nobody wants to be bitter. But they are. Failure to forgive damages life. Forgiveness gives life. Literally. The American psychologist Frederic Luskin supervised a forgiveness project and discovered that forgiveness reduces anger, depression, and stress, and gives feelings of hope, compassion, and self-confidence. Therefore, his conclusion was that forgiveness is good for your relationships and good for your health. If we don't forgive, we damage our bodies. But more than that. We also damage our soul. To use the words of religious philosopher Sitsser:

> *Failure to forgive is like a fire smoldering in your stomach, like smoke that suffocates the soul. It is destructive, because it is treacherous. Sometimes it flares up in the form of a bitter judgment or tantrums. But often, it is happy, living in the background, where it quietly and unnoticed performs its deadly work.*

Nobody gets through life unscathed. You are hit hard and get wounded. Whether they are dormant or forgotten, sooner or later, these wounds wake up. And then we realize that they did more to us than we thought. The blows that we have been dealt still hurt. We still think that they are mean. We are still indignant about the injustice that we have suffered. And we are still angry. That is when it is important for us to realize that forgiveness is the path along which these feelings of anger drain away, and that the stinging pain can be healed. Only the path of forgiveness can prevent the journey from boy to man from being interrupted, and can keep us from getting stuck in bitterness. Only the path of forgiveness can prevent our zest for life, our work ethic, our friendships, our marriage, and even our understanding of God from being characterized by injury.

Joseph and Jesus

Suppose that we want to be like Joseph, that we choose forgiveness. Where do we get the strength? There is just one reason why we should choose the path of Jesus. And the reason is that Jesus chose this path first. For us. Just like Joseph, Jesus was His Father's favourite. Just like Joseph, Jesus watched the herd of His Father. Just like Joseph, Jesus was sent to his brothers, hated by his brothers, sold by his brothers for the price of a slave. Just like Joseph, Jesus was tied up, falsely accused, imprisoned with two others, one of whom was rescued, the other not. Just like Joseph, Jesus started his service to the people when he was 30 years old. Just like Joseph, Jesus was elevated through suffering, and he saved a people. Just like Joseph, Jesus forgave those who had hurt Him. As with Joseph, God used what had been done to Jesus for good, to break open the path of forgiveness, to realize a situation in which we could find forgiveness with God, to realize a situation in which others can find forgiveness with us.

Paul summarizes beautifully it with the words:

> Get rid of all bitterness, rage and anger, brawling
> and slander, along with every form of malice. Be

> *kind and compassionate to one another, forgiving*
> *each other, just as in Christ, God forgave you.*
> *Follow God's example, therefore, as dearly loved*
> *children, and walk in the way of love, just as*
> *Christ loved us and gave Himself up for us as a*
> *fragrant offering and sacrifice to God. (Ephesians*
> *4:31 – 5:2)*

Forgive. It is the road to healing. It is the road to living a lighter life.

16

The empty egg

At length he [the Cardinal] raised his head,
fixed his eagle look upon that loyal, open,
and intelligent countenance, read upon that
face, furrowed with tears, all the sufferings
its possessor [d'Artagnan] had endured in the
course of a month, and reflected for the third or
fourth time how much there was in that youth of
twenty-one years before him, and what resources
his activity, his courage, and his shrewdness
might offer to a good master.

ALEXANDRE DUMAS

Last week, I (Theo) took my son Manuel to school in the car, together with my daughter Rosan. On our way home, it started pouring. Then, the right windscreen wiper broke. Very inconvenient. Through a blur of water, you look into the world, which suddenly looks completely different. Your image distorts. It becomes difficult to calculate distances, and the only thing that you can do is hope that you're driving straight. Since I thought that it would be something that was hard to fix, I decided to keep driving home.

Fortunately, the right windscreen wiper still worked. So there I was, halfway over the passenger seat (something you sometimes see with young men driving fast cars) to be a somewhat responsible participant in traffic. Curves to the right were no problem. The leftward roundabout, however, was a serious challenge. I practically had to climb onto my dashboard to be able to see the curve. Fortunately, there was just one left curve to go, and we made it home safely. I was thankful for that, not least because Rosan was in the car with me.

"Why are things the way they are?"

I (Theo) was talking to a man in the prime of his life. He told me about the moment that his windscreen wiper broke. Suddenly, things weren't so clear any more. His view became blurred. "If the kingdom of God is truly upon us, why is it so hard to see? Why does everything have to be so difficult? Why are things the way they are? Is there no other way? Clearer, for instance. Is there no doubt in your mind that Jesus is King? Because, what if it all turns out to be one big joke?" And someone else said: "I have been running around for years to make a difference in the lives of people and situations in the world. Meanwhile, I am at a point at which I wonder: 'Is there any use to it? What meaning does it have in the bigger picture of life?'"

Every man runs the risk of reaching a point where it rains and the windscreen wiper breaks. You wake up, and you randomly ask yourself what difference it makes whether or not you get out of bed. You're at work, and suddenly, you get sick of the never-ending flow of emails, compelling voicemails, appointments, and text messages. You are among friends, but you lack the energy. You have been wanting to switch jobs for years, but you feel like you've stepped onto the escalator leading to the basement. Where did my childhood friends go? How deep do I want to go to realize my ideals? Is this sense of loneliness normal? And also: Where is that abundant life that Jesus promised us? Where is God when I need Him so badly? "The joy of the Lord is your strength," they say. But why then do I experience so little of both? Do I even have time left for spiritual matters? It seems as if others are doing far better than I am. Are they ever disappointed in themselves? Why does life seem to get more and more complex? I always thought that my worries would change into feelings of detachment and freedom over the years. But they're not.

And suddenly, your view of reality blurs. The direction you were heading in is no longer as clear as it was. And you need to perform all kinds of stunts to take the curves of life. It doesn't feel good. Also, because you have a responsibility to the people in the back seat, the fact that you feel lost also endangers others.

Serious signals

Men are usually very skilled at ignoring these kinds of signals. We are simply too busy, and as soon as things quieten down, and we have more time for ourselves, our friends, or our family, things will work out fine. Still, deep down inside, we know that these questions are signals of deeper feelings. And subconsciously, we know very well what is really going on. The thing is, though, that we don't spend enough time listening to our inner self. The signals remind us of the fact that the majority of life doesn't work out the way we had expected it to. Do you recognize that feeling? "Life usually doesn't do what I had expected it to do." And much harder to accept: The same seems to apply to God sometimes. God does not do what I had expected Him to do.

Seven endless miles

With drooping shoulders, a slow pace, and immersed in a heated discussion, two men walk along the dusty path of Jerusalem to Emmaus. The seven miles feel endless. They feel one warning sign after another emerging from within their subconscious. They feel one question after another popping up. And they know exactly what they are feeling: disappointment. Because things are not going as they had expected them to go. And even more difficult: God hasn't done what they had expected Him to do. You can sense the confusion. "We had expected Jesus to chase away the Romans and to bring liberation and recovery. Until the very last moment, we hoped that Jesus would come down from the cross. We had all our hope invested in Him. But the Romans are still here, and Jesus is dead. It almost seems as if God doesn't know what He is doing. That He has lost control. And sometimes it even feels as if He is playing a game with us. That He has abandoned us."

The men of God had prophesied fiercely about the coming Messiah. Thousands of men, women, and children, like you and me, had eagerly awaited the man who would return life to what it was supposed to be. He had indeed come, and in a way that nobody had expected. But somewhere along the way, things went wrong. Things went differently. And now He is dead.

The village of Emmaus, a spot on the map

We have to be careful when things don't go the way that we had anticipated, when God doesn't do what we want. We have to be really careful when disappointment becomes dominant. When that happens, we start running, figuratively speaking. We settle. We try to avoid the people who have disappointed us and the places where those disappointments happened. We try to avoid situations in which we can get disappointed. And we say: never again. Before we know it, we're on the road to Emmaus.

The village of Emmaus is nothing more than a spot, nothing more than an insignificant dot on the largest world map you've ever seen. A needle in a haystack. If you didn't know that it was there, you'd have passed it before you even knew you had found it. Emmaus. It symbolizes a life that is nothing more than a shadow of what it could have been. Heading to Emmaus, that is our natural response to disappointment: You want to withdraw and tend to make your life really small.

A nine-gallon bucket

The bushel also forms an illustration of what disappointment does. Jesus talks about this in the Sermon on the Mount:

> You are the light of the world. A town built on a hill cannot be hidden. Neither do people light a lamp and put it under a bowl. Instead they put it on its stand, and it gives light to everyone in the house. In the same way, let your light shine before others, that they may see your good deeds and glorify your Father in heaven. (Matthew 5:14–16)

215

The bushel is sort of a nine-gallon bucket, used by men to measure the right amount of wheat. Jesus noted that nobody would place a lamp underneath such a bucket, because the light would go out, and nobody would be able to enjoy it.

What disappointment does

Both the spot Emmaus and the bushel paint a striking image of what disappointment does. Disappointment makes us run to the tiny town of Emmaus. Once we get there, we crawl under a bushel. Disappointment drains the life right out of us. Our heart turns off. We no longer expect too much from life, in order to prevent ourselves from being disappointed. We don't ask too much of God, because last time it didn't work out. We start being annoyed by happy people, because all that excessive joy amounts to nothing. A little more thinking and a little less feeling wouldn't hurt anyone. And when our heart dies out, our light no longer shines for others. It gets darker around us. People in our surroundings start to notice. You start withdrawing. Eventually, disappointment leads to living underneath a bucket. The life expectation dies out. Zest for life and exuberance are left smouldering. All you have left is survival. And meanwhile, Jesus has become a Stranger:

> *As they talked and discussed these things with each other, Jesus himself came up and walked along with them; but they were kept from recognizing him. (Luke 24:15–16)*

How the Stranger helps

Disappointment cries out for healing. It is touching to see how the Stranger heals two people heading for Emmaus. He approaches them, asks questions, and allows them to talk. Then, out of love, He puts his finger on the sore spot: "You are suffering from a lack of faith. It has two causes. You are too worried to be able to think straight, and you know too little of the Bible to be able to understand God's intention." Then, Jesus starts explaining the Scriptures. And finally, He completes the healing process by opening the eyes of their hearts to His presence: "Then their eyes were opened and they recognized him" (Luke 24:31).

To their surprise, the Stranger is no Stranger at all. Jesus isn't dead. He's alive. And He is here. It appears that God knows exactly what He is doing.

We are very curious about exactly how this took place. Perhaps they saw His hands or recognized His voice. We don't know. The way Jesus reveals His presence is a big secret, about which we can only say that it happened. That applied to the men walking to Emmaus. And it still applies today. Jesus revealed that He was there, and with that, they had been healed.

Issues with the cross

The problem of the two men heading for Emmaus was that they focused too much on the cross. They focused too much on a wall of suffering. They didn't understand that suffering can have a place in God's plan. This is extremely understandable. The cross is very difficult. A Musketeer says about the cross:

> *The cross is so shocking. I was eating at*
> *someone's place, and there was a cross there.*
> *That ruins my appetite. The cross is so rude.*
> *The idea that the cross is also there because of*
> *me bothers me greatly. Dealing with the cross*
> *is so difficult, because it is feels so unfair. Grace*
> *is so incomprehensible. It is so big. You keep*
> *feeling that something has to be behind it. You*
> *keep feeling that, eventually, you have to do*
> *something.*

The cross is hard to deal with. Staring at the cross means staring at a wall of suffering. The only way to look at the cross without it overwhelming you is by regarding it in the light of the resurrection. It is Sunday that gives Friday a purpose. Only Sunday morning can give Friday afternoon sense and meaning. Without the resurrection, our faith would still be without substance. Only because the grave is empty can we can sing about the cross.

Philip, the boy who was so different

Someone who understood this very well was little Philip. Philip, who was born with Down's syndrome, attended a Sunday school class with a group of children, all about eight years old. The other children had difficulties accepting Philip, because he was "different". But the creative efforts of the teachers caused them to start taking care of Philip and to allow him to be part of the group. But still, with some reservations. On the Sunday after Easter, the Sunday school teacher brought boxes that had once held stockings. They had the shape of large eggs and were used for a fun activity for the class. Everyone received an egg. The assignment was to take it into the spring sun and look for something that symbolizes new life. The intention was for all children to store their symbol in the egg-shaped box. Subsequently, they would review all their findings together. Back in the classroom, the table was full of "eggs". The Sunday school teacher opened them, one by one. Some held a flower; others held a butterfly or a leaf. With the children making noises of excitement, the teacher opened the next one. There was nothing in it. The children exclaimed that it was stupid and unfair. They were indignant that someone had not followed the instructions. Then Philip softly whispered: "That one is mine."

The children responded by exclaiming that there was always something wrong with what Philip did. But Philip stressed: "There is nothing in it. I did that on purpose. That was my intention. It is... empty. It is empty. The grave was empty!"

Then, everyone fell silent.

From that moment on, the children fully embraced Philip and he was accepted. He died not long afterwards, from an infection that most "normal" children would easily survive. At his funeral, the children of the Sunday school class and their teacher walked towards the coffin at the front of the church that contained Philip's body. Not with flowers. Each child was holding an egg-shaped box that once used to contain stockings and placed it on top of the coffin...

Empty.

"The empty egg" gives hope

The resurrection of Jesus Christ sheds its beautiful light on the cross and inspires people to live. It provides energy. To us, it is strange to read that the men who were heading to Emmaus immediately returned to Jerusalem after their encounter with Jesus. All of a sudden, they are no longer heading to Emmaus. Their life has taken a turn. Those who are wise also notice it, and as they shake their heads, you can hear them say, "Irresponsible. How ignorant can you be? It is dark. It is late. The road is long and lonely. There were robbers and scum all around. That's asking for trouble. Just stay where you are." But the two men don't hear it. They are long gone. They are flying. To become participants in the biggest adventure in the history of the world.

What do you do if life doesn't unfold the way that you had anticipated? What do you do if God doesn't do what you had expected Him to? When disappointment comes knocking on your door, and Jesus seems to be a Stranger?

Do you run to Emmaus? Do you quit in disappointment?

Or do you allow Jesus to heal you? Do you keep having hope? Do you allow God the Father to shape your heart? To make you the man He wants you to be?

Titanium

Recently, I (Theo) was talking to Hansie. If there's anyone who – humanly speaking – had every reason to quit in disappointment, it is him. Hansie is a trauma worker, rides the ambulance, has seen far too many people die, and knows what it feels like to be involved in an accident. Nearly eight years ago – he was 30 years old at the time – a bike crash almost killed him. The bone in his upper leg had been shattered, although his muscles and nerves were virtually intact, which was a sheer miracle. For five and a half years, Hansie was unable to walk. Thanks to countless operations, titanium, rehabilitation, and crutches, he started being able to get places on his own again about two years ago. Five and a half years of not being able to walk, and not being able to do the things you love to do... that requires a lot of patience from the family, gives you far too much time to think, and provides far too much opportunity to quit in disappointment. Still, Jesus did not become a stranger to Hansie. Hansie kept having hope. He chose to have himself shaped by the Father. "I see it as a cathartic time. God has shut me down, and He gave me a new direction in that period. God knows what's best. He doesn't provide a comfortable life. He doesn't care about what you have; he cares about what you give. I keep having faith in the fact that God knows what He's doing and that He has control. No matter what happens."

Not a full stop, but a comma

The empty grave is God's remedy for disappointment. The empty grave reminds us of the wonderful fact that God hasn't lost control. It reminds us of the fact that God knows exactly what He is doing and knows more about life than we do. He didn't just allow Pilate to do what he wanted by accident, but chose the battle against Satan. He didn't leave the Romans below by accident, but decided to eliminate far more dangerous beings. He didn't postpone the liberation of Israel by accident, but included it in the total liberation of humanity in a way that was unthought of: through suffering. God knows more about life than we do. Death is not a full stop, but the most wonderful comma in the history of the world. The sentence doesn't end. The resurrection is the beginning of a wonderful new chapter.

It touches us once we realize what it is that the Bible says about the power that awoke Jesus Christ from the dead. The Spirit power is the result of faith in us. Now. We only need to look at the two heading for Emmaus one time in order to see what that power can do. The resurrection inspired. Hope sustains life, makes our hearts ignite, turns our eyes sharp. Jesus is there. Our feet want to get moving.

Just like those two.

17

Winning, German-style

Upon which M. d'Artagnan the elder girded his own sword round his son, kissed him tenderly on both cheeks, and gave him his benediction.

ALEXANDRE DUMAS

There will be a time when your heart stops beating, your blood stops flowing, your diaphragm contracts for the very last time.

What will you leave behind?

Leonard Woolf, an important British politician, concludes his autobiography with the words:

Looking back at the age of eighty-eight over the fifty-seven years of my political work in England, knowing what I aimed at and the results, meditating on the history of Britain and the world since 1914, I see clearly that I achieved practically nothing. The world today and the history of the human anthill during the past five to seven years would be exactly the same

*if I had played Ping-Pong instead of sitting on
committees and writing books and memoranda.
I have therefore to make a rather ignominious
confession to myself and everyone who reads this
book, that I have in a long life ground through
between 150,000 and 200,000 hours of perfectly
useless work.*

Nobody wants to reach the conclusion at the end of their life that they might as well have played ping-pong. It is a universal desire of man to leave a mark on existence, to make a difference, to sense that his life has mattered. We want to be remembered. Some make television shows; others write books. Some start a company, others a foundation. And others try to make something of themselves live on through their children. But all from the same desire, to let the world know one simple thing: I was here.

Alexander the Great, the man who kept getting smaller

When Harmke and I lived in Thessaloniki, we frequently strolled along the boulevard. Amid all the beautiful remains from the classical era, there was a statue of Alexander III of Macedonia, sitting on a horse. After the murder of his father, he became king at a very young age. He set things in order in his own country and then took a 45,000-man army to battle the powerful Persian Empire. He proved to be a brilliant strategist and beat every army he encountered. When he was 25, the Persians succumbed and were forced to acknowledge Alexander as their ruler. Alexander III became Alexander the Great. Eventually, his empire stretched from Egypt to India, and his influence was unprecedented. Greek was declared the official language, and trade was flourishing.

So far, so good. Humanly speaking, he played an awesome match. But Alexander the Great had one problem. He was so involved in the here and now, and with getting bigger and bigger, that he forgot to invest in the next generation. At the age of 32, he died without having a proper successor. The consequences were disastrous. His friends battled for the main position and killed each other one by one. Before long, the strongest generals seized power, and the empire was broken into four parts. In the turmoil, many of Alexander's loved ones died, including his mother, his wife, his (half) brother, his (half) sister, and the majority of his best officers. Alexander's vision for the present was legendary, but his lack of vision for the future was baffling and his legacy was disastrous.

How do you prepare your legacy?

What memory are you building? How you live determines how you will be remembered. What you do with the most precious gift you have ever been given – your life – determines what your legacy will look like. Although some live to be 100, for their legacy it would hardly matter, because they only live for themselves, and it wouldn't affect anyone. A long life doesn't necessarily mean anything. It is how you live that matters. That is decisive for your legacy. What are you planning to leave behind for your loved ones, for the community you are part of, for the world?

Being able to hand over a positive legacy to the next generation proves to be less obvious than you'd think. we can study the beginnings and the endings of hundreds of lives in the Bible. About three-quarters of them don't end well, and they don't seize the opportunity to launch the next generation on the right track.

Cockiness

Take Gideon, for instance. He played an excellent first half. After a somewhat hesitant start, a cruel and rapacious enemy was quickly eliminated. Peace returned to the country for a period of 40 years. Children played outside. Women could finally cook the most delicious meals again. Men got satisfaction from their work again. When the clock hit half-time, Gideon was leading by several points. But in the second half, things started to go wrong. Gideon deceived the people into idolatry, got cocky, and started behaving like a king. He seduced one woman after another, and fathered 70 sons. He named one of them Abimelech, which means "father is king", a very expressive name. After Gideon's death, the Israelites started to follow the Baals once again, resulting in a gruesome power struggle between his sons. Abimelech killed all his brothers on the same rock, burnt people alive, murdered entire cities, and ended up with a crushed skull himself.

Wisdom and wealth mean nothing

And what about Solomon? He also played a promising first half. He asked God for wisdom and received it. He undertook gigantic construction projects and completed the temple. The inauguration of that temple was a historic moment. God's glory descended in a mighty manner. And the trade industry flourished, too. Life was good. Solomon also cashed in on his wisdom in the literary field. He was responsible for 3,000 proverbs, 1,005 songs, and several scientific works about botany and zoology. Things were going great, and 1 Kings 10 therefore says:

> *King Solomon was greater in riches and wisdom*
> *than all the other kings of the earth. The whole*
> *world sought audience with Solomon to hear*
> *the wisdom God had put in his heart. (1 Kings*
> *10:23–24)*

At the halfway point, Solomon appeared to be heading for a rich legacy. But then there's the second half:

> *He had seven hundred wives of royal birth and*
> *three hundred concubines, and his wives led him*
> *astray. As Solomon grew old, his wives turned*
> *his heart after other gods, and his heart was not*
> *fully devoted to the Lord his God, as the heart of*
> *David his father had been. (1 Kings 11:3–4)*

And:

> *Solomon did evil in the eyes of the Lord; he did*
> *not follow the Lord completely, as David his*
> *father had done. (1 Kings 11:6)*

The dream bursts into pieces. The legacy shrivels.

Why the second half is so important

As we were writing this, the World Cup Soccer 2010 event was in full swing. The Netherlands had beaten Brazil in the quarter-finals. At the end of the first half, the score was 0–1. But in the second half, the ball ended up in the Brazilian goal, the momentum switched, and the Netherlands won. Final score 2–1. The Netherlands was in ecstasy. Two hundred million Brazilians and 16 million

Dutchmen witnessed the truth: A game isn't over until the second half has been played. Finally, we won, German-style.

This illustrates the lives of Gideon and Solomon: A good first half is not enough. The half-time score means nothing. It is about the entire game. Gideon conquered 135,000 men. Under Solomon, the empire flourished. But Gideon got cocky and decided to rest on the laurels of his victory. His son Abimelech was a disaster. Solomon forgot the rules of the game, no longer lost his heart to God but to women, and lapsed into idolatry. His son Rehoboam was a horror, and the kingdom cracked and broke in two. Both Gideon and Solomon lost their inspiration, their passion for the Lord, and failed to think about the next generation. Their sons brought tragedy to the people.

Remaining faithful until the end

Ending well isn't a given. Handing over a rich legacy isn't, either. It requires a life that is devoted to the Lord until the very end. It requires full inspiration in serving God, until the moment when we will stumble into eternity in exhaustion, and we will hear the Lord say:

> *Well done, good and faithful servant! You have been faithful with a few things; I will put you in charge of many things. Come and share your master's happiness! (Matthew 25:23)*

Only then will the job be done here. And not a moment before.

What does the path to a rich legacy look like?

It starts with living within the perspective of eternity. The deep awareness that a wonderful legacy awaits us in heaven will inspire us to build a wonderful legacy here on earth. Paul writes about the future glory that we will receive:

> *I consider that our present sufferings are not worth comparing with the glory that will be revealed in us. (Romans 8:18)*

> *The creation itself will be liberated from its bondage to decay and brought into the freedom and glory of the children of God. (Romans 8:21)*

Based on this section, we sometimes are afraid that, after spending less than a second in eternity, we'll be exclaiming, "Oh, my God, why? Why was I so selfish? Why didn't I give more, share more, do more? Why didn't I look more like Jesus? Living for my loved ones. Thinking about my fellow men. Giving to the less fortunate. Why did I not focus on You more? Why did I give myself to things, and why didn't I invest more in people? Why did I live for things that last for only 80 years? Why did I not pursue eternal treasures?" An important answer to these questions is that we often forget that we don't belong to ourselves. That is why Paul stresses the following:

> *For none of us lives for ourselves alone, and none of us dies for ourselves alone. If we live, we live for the Lord; and if we die, we die for the Lord. So, whether we live or die, we belong to the Lord. (Romans 14:7–8)*

Whose are you?

As soon as we start thinking that who we become and what we have is the result of our personal efforts, everything starts revolving around personal success. As soon as we acknowledge that all we are and all we have is the property of the Lord, we begin giving to others because living for the Lord is done by giving to others. The best way to serve your Lord is to serve other people with your best. Serving is investing in people. Investing in people means building a rich legacy. From a deep awareness that we aren't ours, there is a growing awareness that, at one point, we will need to explain to the Lord what we did with our lives:

We will all stand before God's judgment seat.
It is written: "'As surely as I live,' says the Lord,
'every knee will bow before me; every tongue
will acknowledge God.'" So then, each of us will
give an account of ourselves to God. (Romans
14:10b–12)

People tend to be very good at paying attention to each other, especially when it concerns things that others don't do correctly. Based on the words of Paul, it seems wiser simply to focus on your own life. Every person will be given plenty of opportunity to explain to the Lord what they did with their life and why they lived it the way that they lived it. That may seem scary, but it's not necessary to be scared. It is an inspiration for a life of giving. God sees it, appreciates it, and in time, we will be able to discuss it with Him. This perspective will help us to focus on the things that truly matter:

*Therefore do not let what you know is good
be spoken of as evil. For the kingdom of God
is not a matter of eating and drinking, but of
righteousness, and peace and joy in the Holy
Spirit. (Romans 14:16–17)*

Draining or contributing

The kingdom of God is not about success. The question
will not be: "How many people did you manage to impress
with the sum of all your performances? Who only feels like
a ghost in your shadow? What tricks can you do, and what
has it got you? What car did you drive?" The question will
be: "Did you harm the good that God gave you, or did you
make it flourish? Is the world a place with more justice,
more peace, and more joy because you lived? Did you drain
it or contribute to it? Were you a giver or a taker?"

A Musketeer says:

*The choices I made were not always of eternal
value, in general. They were more about the
question of how I could get a big house and
beautiful things as quickly as possible. I took my
pride from the designer clothes I wore, and I
felt like a big shot in my massive car. If I had it
my way, everyone on the freeway would need to
move over because I was coming. This realization
hit me so hard during the XCC that I thanked
God, crying, that He had opened my eyes after
years of going to the church. That I was given the
opportunity to see that the choices I made would
only be relevant until I died, and not a second
beyond that.*

Personal success, or meaning to others

You can lose your life, even before you die, by making choices that "will only last you until death". Why do many people – even the most successful ones – often feel miserable, bored, or unfulfilled? Because they focus on "personal success" and not on "meaning to others". And that approach doesn't work. It costs you your life. In a certain way, this is a dynamic that God has placed in the cosmos. The motion of getting and grabbing and seizing and draining, by definition, gives you zero satisfaction. People who don't realize this will keep thinking that the lack of satisfaction is caused by the fact that they don't have enough personal success. But the opposite is true. The more success that you achieve, the greater the hunger will be for more success. This endless pursuit leads to loss of life. You can lose your life even before you die. Jesus says:

> *For whoever wants to save their life will lose it,*
> *but whoever loses their life for me and for the*
> *gospel will save it. What good is it for someone*
> *to gain the whole world, yet forfeit their soul?*
> *(Mark 8:35–36)*

Some people are like a lump of stone. When you hit it with a hammer, splinters will be knocked off. Others are like a sponge. You need to wring them out to get something from them. And yet others are like a source. They keep giving, they keep sharing, they keep blessing. Jesus says the best way is a life of giving. It is the paradox of the gospel. Give as much as possible, and you will have as much as possible. Not just you, but the next generation as well. How is that possible? Because you cannot outgive God. As long as you give, God gives. And He always gives more.

Giving lives on in the next generation.

Giving makes your legacy grow, because you exchange the pursuit of personal success for a holy desire for meaning in the lives of others.

What can we give the next generation?

Encouragement, for instance. We can ask ourselves: Who will feel more competent because of my words? If you think about who has affected your life the most up until now, you'll probably discover that these are the people who have encouraged you mostly with their words. Proverbs 10:21 states: "The lips of the righteous nourish many."

Which people have been encouraged by the food of your words? Which people walk around with more courage, more focus, more passion, and more direction, only because you have encouraged them with words of truth, strength, and love?

John Wendel and his sisters

We can also think about this question: What am I doing with what I have? How can you use the material and financial resources you have to an optimal extent for the next generation?

John Wendel and his sisters are among the saddest people who have ever lived. Despite the fact that they had inherited a fortune from their parents, they hardly spent anything. They did everything in their power to keep their money to themselves whenever possible. John convinced his sisters not to marry, and, together, they lived in the same house in New York City for 50 years. When the last sister died in 1931, the total value of her assets was more than $100 million dollars. The only dress she owned was one she had made herself. She had worn it for 25 years. The Wendels are similar to the man about whom Jesus speaks in the parable in Luke 12. God's response is this:

> "You fool! This very night your life will be
> demanded from you. Then who will get what you
> have prepared for yourself?" This is how it will be
> with whoever stores up things for themselves but
> is not rich toward God. (Luke 12:20–21)

"Men are not big talkers"

Another way to invest in the future generation is through insight. Ask yourself: Who benefits from what I have learned? We all know the saying: "Men are not big talkers." In many cases, that's right... and that's a shame. Because the risk is that much of the wisdom, knowledge, and insight that we have gained through trial and error, loss and victory, is lost to the next generation of men. That is a pity. What has God taught you that is valuable to others? Christian author Gordon MacDonald describes the loss of a son who wonders why his dad has never shown more of his heart, why his father didn't help him understand life better, understand more about the struggle of a man. It could have been so helpful. The son writes to his father:

> Oh, my father. Why didn't you open your real
> heart when I was looking? Why did you only
> show me strength when I needed to know it was

okay to be weak? My father, why did you never tell me that you were sometimes so crushed that you wanted to run away, that you knew terrible disappointment when people let you down, that you may even have got angry at God once or twice, that you grieved because you didn't know your father either, that you tasted the anguish of loneliness and wished for a friend... or two, and that you may even have doubted your own manhood now and then?

The most heroic second half ever

One of the most substantial ways to be a blessing for the next generation lies in this question: Will I have pointed the way to God? Paul was a man who – in the end – gave every last drop of his energy for this goal. Initially, he played a lousy first half. His zeal for God and the arrival of His kingdom was significant, but it was misguided. Many men, women, and children, all followers of Jesus, were killed because of Saul. But God intervened. And Paul played the most heroic second half a man can play. Right before the final whistle of his life, while reflecting on intense years of service for the King, we hear him say to Timothy: "I have fought the good fight, I have finished the race, I have kept the faith" (2 Timothy 4:7).

Paul ended well, and he left behind a rich legacy. He tirelessly alerted people to Christ. Countless people found faith in Jesus. Churches emerged everywhere, Christianity bloomed, and cities changed. To date, generation after generation has reaped the benefits of his life.

Three Musketeers

This past summer, I was in South Africa for my work with Athletes in Action. There, I encountered some remarkable men, who, entirely in line with Paul – but each in their own way – pointed others to the way to God. Three of these men are Norman, Ewald, and Henley. Their lives illustrate what it means to invest in the next generation.

Overwhelmed by kindness

Until three years ago, 57-year-old Norman was a bitter racist. He hated black people, and he hated children. Resentment was deeply embedded in his life. Born with a muscle condition, Norman had been an outcast ever since he was a child. At the age of six, he started limping. Childhood photos showed an energetic and frolicking brother and sister, and a cowering boy sitting on his father's shoulders because he was too weak to walk: little Norman. Twice, he seriously pursued love, once as a teen and once in his twenties. Both times, it was a failure. "I curse the day I was born!" Norman's words hit his mother like lightning. She was next to him when he yelled those words. Norman found work in the diamond mines, became an expert in the field of weaponry, and lived a life that goes along with that. Until three years ago. For some time, he had been noticing that his neighbours "went somewhere" every Sunday morning. One day, Norman decided to ask them where they were going. "Why don't you join us? We'll be happy to show you where we go," the neighbours replied. And so, Norman found his way to church, without even noticing it at first. As soon as he set foot in the building, something happened that must be a nightmare for a racist who hates black people and children. A group of black children enthusiastically ran up to him to greet him. He tried to find repellent words and gestures, but to no avail. The children gathered around him and overwhelmed him with kindness. He received something that he had never been given before. Deep inside, something happened to him. Norman had become a new man in an instant. Later, he disposed of all of his weapons. He had no time for that any more. He now invests all his energy in working with the disabled and visiting prisoners. He wants to be like Christ for them.

Absent fathers

A couple of days later, I decided to look up Ewald. Via dusty roads, I arrived at the slum. Ewald, a small guy, 38 years old, walked up to me and gave me a heartfelt welcome. I looked around and saw three small old caravans, one awning, and an improvised area that serves as a kitchen. This is where Ewald lives, together with his wife and three foster children. Why? Why would you give up your excellent job, sell your house and possessions, and decide to live in a rough and dangerous place? What drives you to do that? "One night, my wife and I were watching a movie, *Second Chance*. God spoke to us. We had no choice but to make drastic choices. It is a privilege to follow Jesus and to be able to do this for him," was the simple answer of Ewald. Then, he told me about the plight of the people in the township. "The two biggest problems here are alcohol and absent fathers. Eighty per cent of the children don't live with their father. The only forms of 'entertainment' these children have are being part of a gang, sniffing glue, and using drugs. We have come here to be among these people, to get these children and teens out of that downward spiral, and to help them to build a dignified existence."

Full stomachs

A short time later, I met Henley. On the surface, he is a hardened man, but his eyes reveal a kind heart. This 40-year-old farmer radically found faith three years ago. "I had my own business, abused my staff when they made mistakes, was constantly bribing people, drank one bottle of whisky a day, and had a bad marriage. During that period, someone gave me a Bible. At home, I smashed the Bible onto the kitchen table in anger. I was furious that someone had dared to give me a Bible. Within six months of that day, my wife told me that I needed to make some changes, or she would seek a divorce. I felt compelled to read the Bible. After one hour of reading, I became a different person. God captured me, and my whole life was turned upside down." As I was talking to Henley, I could hardly imagine that this sympathetic man once didn't see anyone and didn't want to help anyone. Now, he helps everyone that he runs into. In addition to his regular work, he feeds 350 children every day. In doing so, he brings relief to countless families. "Empty stomachs cause children to be beaten and abused, out of feelings of pure frustration and despair. If you give them food, children come home with full stomachs, and they become a source of joy, which brings peace back to the family." Every day, 350 children feel the gospel in their stomachs. Henley invests in the next generation every day, and is building a rich legacy by doing so.

What do you leave behind?

Sir Leonard Woolf ended up disillusioned, and – to his shame – was forced to conclude that he had spent his life doing utterly useless work. Alexander the Great forgot to see beyond his death, and his legacy was disastrous. Gideon and Solomon both played a great first half, but one of them got cocky and the other forgot the rules of the game. Paul started laboriously, but he played a legendary second half and ended well. Norman, Ewald, and Henley are doing a great job. Each of these three abandoned the path of the boy and chose the path of the man. During their journeys, they lost their desire for personal success, thanks to the rip in that hessian sack. Caring for others became the focus of their mission.

And you? What memory are you building? What are you planning to leave behind for your loved ones, for the church you are part of, for the world?

Make your mark on the next generation. Before long, you'll have an eternity to rest.

Epilogue

The man with a mission

Who am I? They often tell me
  I would step from my cell's confinement
  calmly, cheerfully, firmly,
  like a squire from his country-house.

Who am I? They often tell me
  I would talk to my warders
  freely and friendly and clearly,
  as though it were mine to command.

Who am I? They also tell me
  I would bear the days of misfortune
  equably, smilingly, proudly,
  like one accustomed to win.

Am I then really all that which other men tell of?
  Or am I only what I know of myself,
  restless and longing and sick, like a bird in a cage,
  struggling for breath, as though hands were compressing my throat,
  yearning for colours, for flowers, for the voices of birds,
  thirsting for words of kindness, for neighbourliness,
  tossing in expectation of great events,
  powerlessly trembling for friends at an infinite distance,
  weary and empty at praying, at thinking, at making,

faint, and ready to say farewell to it all?

Who am I? This or the other?
 Am I one person today, and tomorrow another?
 Am I both at once? A hypocrite before others,
 and before myself a contemptibly woebegone weakling?
 Or is something within me still like a beaten army,
 fleeing in disorder from victory already achieved?

Who am I? They mock me, these lonely questions of mine.
 Whoever I am, Thou knowest, O God, I am thine!

This prayer was written by Dietrich Bonhoeffer, a German preacher and theologian who lived in Nazi Germany during World War II. He was captured because he helped Jews to escape, and he was subsequently placed in various prisons and concentration camps. Three weeks before the liberation, he was murdered.

Who are you?
 You are a story. You are on an adventure.
 You are on a journey with Jesus. And in that process of life, God shapes you to be the man He intended you to be.
 God doesn't take any shortcuts. Killing a lion once is not enough. The Father uses life itself to shape you into a man. You will bring along the hessian sack. Along the way, you'll be able to say goodbye to the old man; you'll lose the bull, and the potatoes, and the raven. You will find life.
 Who are you?
 The boy with the hessian sack? Or the man with the mission?

Prayers

Prayer of surrender

Lord Jesus Christ, you know me completely.
My past, present, and future are an open book to
   you.
There is nothing I have done that would shock
   you, because you already know.
You understand and know me.
And you want me.
Thank you for your grace. By your word and by
   this book.
I want to know you, and I give you my life.
Come to me, Father. Wash me clean. Fill me.
Possess me. Lead me. Send me.
In Jesus' name,
Amen

Sunday

Father God, supreme Lord,
Thank you for letting me go to your house today,
   for letting me cross the threshold and get closer
   to You.
Give me grace to bring you something – myself.
Fill me with your Spirit, so that I will sing, pray,

and listen in a way that befits someone
saved by you.
Bless our church. Let it be your instrument of
grace for people close and far away.

Monday

Father, be the Lord of everything I do today and
all this week.
Give me a holy fire inside, so I will work diligently
and with love.
Where I dread tasks, I pray for strength, so
that I won't be controlled by laziness, but by
decisiveness.
I pray for new open doors, new opportunities to
serve you.
I pray that I will always see first the person,
and only then the product or the goals or the
problem.
Let me be like a tree, planted by flowing streams,
giving its fruit at the proper time, and with
whom everything succeeds.

Tuesday

Father in heaven, thank you for the wife you have
given me.
Show me how I can honour and serve her as she
deserves.
Give me grace to love her so intensely that she
will bloom as a fresh flower.
Teach me to pray for [the name of your wife], in
such a way that my prayers shall act as a shield

around her.

I pray that you will renew our relationship, that
you will give us new passion for you and for
each other.

Let my words build her up, not break her down.

Make my heart soft for her, so that I will forgive
and see what she needs, even before she has to
ask for it.

Bless our relationship, and let it be a silent
testimony of your love for us all.

Wednesday

Lord Jesus Christ, Son of God, have mercy on us.

Create a clean heart within me and renew me in
a right spirit, so that I will serve and follow you.

Today I declare that you are the first, the foremost
in my life.

Whom do I have in heaven but you? And beside
you, I desire nothing on this earth.

[Give me grace to leave my father and mother
and to unite with my wife.]

Open my heart to friends. Let me be a Jonathan
to a David and give me a Jonathan to protect my
heart.

Lord, you know which potatoes I carry around in
my hessian sack.

Let me know what I can let go of, that I may
follow you in freedom.

Thursday

My Lord Jesus Christ,

Today, I pray to you for the children of this world, asking that you would bless, anoint, and protect them.

I pray particularly for the countless children in need:

the abused, the attacked, the child slaves, the rejected, the homeless, the hungry, the sick — a sea of suffering, an ocean of injustice.

Let your law reign on earth. Let your kingdom come with power.

Bless all those churches and people who help children.

[Introduce yourself to me as my Heavenly Father.

Allow me to "father" my children as you had mercy on me.

Give me grace to bring my children to you.

Give them a heart to know you and to follow you wholeheartedly.

Reveal your work to me, and your glory over my children.]

And I also pray "Maranatha, come, Lord Jesus, come".

Friday

Dear God, free me from the stranglehold of money, sex, and power.

Show me where my will, mindset, and actions are infected with this virus.

Why would I allow my life to be robbed, by the idols of this world?

*Why would I settle for false gods when You, the
Supreme, want to know me?
Give me a heart, Lord, to give, instead of to take.
Make me quick to serve, instead of to rule.
Let my heart be full of love, instead of being
    consumed by lust.
Open my eyes to your goals for my life.
Let me walk honourably, in the light, so pure that
I don't have to hide anything.*

Saturday

*Faithful Father in heaven,
Another week has passed. It went so fast.
Before I knew it, I kept going again, lived too fast.
Although in sight of the mountain, I settled for
    my circles on the lake, the old patterns, the old
    emptiness, my old me.
Thank you, that you, the God of heaven and
    earth, the Father of eternity, visit me.
Renew, yes, rejuvenate my mindset.
Bring me to new life. Through peace. By playing
    some.
Rejuvenate my inner self and reinforce my heart
    with bread and wine.
I want to live slowly today, waiting for my soul,
    for you.*

Sources

1 Why Alexander Supertramp died

Page 21: The story of Chris McCandless is described in Jon Krakauer's *Into the Wild*, 1996, and is available as a movie, also called *Into the Wild*.
Page 23: Jon Krakauer, *Into the Wild*, 1996, p. 85.
Page 23: Jon Krakauer, *Into the Wild*, 1996, pp. 25–26.

2 Preaching for my father

Pages 33–34: Movie quotes all from *Rudy*, 1993.
Page 35: J. Marvin Eisenstadt, *Parental Loss and Genius*, 1978.

3 Thou shalt hate

Page 46: Henri Nouwen, *Jesus*, 2003, p. 44.
Page 54: A.W. Tozer quoted in Mike Bickle, *Passion for Jesus*, 1998, p. 47.

4 Prepared to die

Page 61: Nicky Cruz, *Run Baby Run*, 1969, p. 119.

6 To the other side, while sleeping

Page 90: The story of the Christian in Nazi Germany is told by Mark Stibbe in *Luid en duidelijk*, 2010, p. 10.
Pages 93–94: Max Meyers, *Riding the Heavens*, 2002, pp. 87–88.

7 Hunting like Nimrod

Page 99: J. Oswald Sanders, *Spiritual Leadership*, 1967, p. 17.
Page 101: The story of Stan Dale is told in Don Richardson, *Lords of the Earth*, 1997.

8 Three musketeers

Pages 114–15: Søren Kierkegaard, *The Passionless Age*, 2006, p. 122.
Page 117: Oswald Chambers, *My Utmost for His Highest*, 2003, p. 340.

11 The theological significance of the ostrich

Page 152: Mark Twain, *The Adventures of Tom Sawyer*, 2007, p. 138.
Pages 156: Movie quote from *Fight Club*, 1999.
Pages 158: Meister Eckhardt, quoted in David James Duncan, *God Laughs and Plays*, 2006, p. 4.
Pages 160–61: Umberto Eco, *The Name of the Rose*, 2004, p. 495.

12 The slaughter of Olaf the Ox

Page 166: General Dallaire, quoted in John Rucyahana, *The Bishop of Rwanda*, 2007, p. 132.
Pages 168–69: C.S. Lewis, *The Screwtape Letters*, 1982, p. 41.

14 Fleeing towards the sun

Pages 191–92: Jerry Sitsser, *A Grace Disguised*, 2005, p. 34.
Page 192: Jerry Sitsser, *A Grace Disguised*, 2005, p. 99.
Page 192: Jerry Sitsser, *A Grace Disguised*, 2005, p. 100.
Page 193: Manu Keirse, *Helpen bij verlies en verdriet*, 2003, p. 54.
Page 193: Manu Keirse, *Helpen bij verlies en verdriet*, 2003, p. 54.
Page 195: Gordon MacDonald, *When Men Think Private Thoughts*, 2008, p. 137.
Page 197: For more information about the fundraiser for cancer, see http://deelnemers.alpe-dhuzes.nl/.

15 I forgive you, asshole

Page 199: Julie Fitness, www.psychologiemagazine.nl/web/Dossiers/Archief/Vergeven-doe-je-voor-jezelf.htm.
Page 200: Neil Anderson, *Victory Over the Darkness*, 1999, p. 234.
Pages 203–204: Johan and Janneke are not their real names; pseudonyms have been used for reasons of privacy.

Page 208: Frederic Luskin, www.psychologiemagazine.nl/web/Dossiers/
Archief/Vergeven-doe-je-voor-jezelf.htm.
Page 208: Jerry Sitsser, *A Grace Disguised*, 2005, p. 139.

17 Winning, German-style

Pages 234–35: Gordon MacDonald, *When Men Think Private Thoughts*,
2008, p. 120.

Epilogue: The man with a mission

Pages 240–41: Dietrich Bonhoeffer, *Letters and Papers from Prison*,
enlarged edition, 1971, pp. 309–310.

Study material

Study material has been developed for this book. The questions and assignments serve as a tool to help process the contents of the chapters in person. We recommend reading this book simultaneously with other men and to discuss the study material afterwards. Sharing from heart to heart always leads to remarkable results and reinforces friendships in a powerful way.

The material can be downloaded for free, at www.de4emusketier.nl.

Acknowledgments

Dear Harmke and Ruth, thank you for your love and support. Without you, this book would not have existed. You make us each feel like more of a man! You are worth dying for.

We would like to thank both of our fathers. Our life chapters are intertwined. We love you.

Jan, Pieter, Jannes, and Johannes, we love seeking out adventure with you guys. You have guts. Thank you!

Derek, Eugene, Jaap, Janneke, and Marco, thank you for your efforts in going through the manuscript! Your contribution was extremely valuable.

Ernst, thank you so much for taking a chance on us. We admire your creativity and patience.

We would also like to thank all Musketeers who have submitted a personal story.

About the authors

Henk about Theo

I wish I was a little more like Theo. He is a wonderful man. Physically, he is very manly: an athletic body, great at swimming, and an outdoor enthusiast. Yes, on the outside, he's great. And that goes double for the inside. He has character. He perseveres, has integrity, is gentle. He is someone I trust blindly.

His wife Harmke and their three children, Manuel (4), Rosan (2), and Luca (0), are blessed with Theo as a husband and father. Theo succeeded me as the leader of Athletes in Action (AIA) Netherlands. Over the past year, he has courageously carried out this responsibility. AIA is now doing much better than when I handed it to him thanks to his excellent leadership.

Writing this book together was wonderful. The lessons from The 4th Musketeer Wilderness are now reflected on paper, in the hope that even more men will be blessed by this men's movement.

If you're ever looking for an inspiring speaker for a men's day, training class, or church service, please feel free to email Theo at theo.van.den.heuvel@solcon.nl.

Theo about Henk

I always love spending time with Henk. He inspires! Because Henk loves life. Like no other, I know him as the man of the creative initiative. A pioneer with guts. A sharp, quick, and original thinker, I always fully enjoy the surprise and dynamics that leads to. Moreover, Henk has a beautiful heart – friendly, turbulent, spirited, courageous – a heart that wants to be touched deeply both by beauty and distress.

Henk always speaks of his wife Ruth and their three children Manoa (5), Emma (3), and Chris (1) with love and admiration. They are happy to have a husband and father who chooses them over everything else.

I was introduced to Henk when he was leading Athletes in Action (AIA) Netherlands as its founder. Now, he is pastor for municipality development of the Free Evangelical Church in Zwolle, an inspiring speaker, and the author of *De Leerling* ["The Student"] and *Geboren om te vliegen* ["Born to Fly"], among other works.

Writing this book was an adventure in itself in the story that we live. We hope that it will take many men further in shaping their own story and mission in life.

Henk is a popular (international) speaker. Should you want to invite him to speak, you can do so by sending an email to henk.stoorvogel@home.nl.

The 4th Musketeer

4M is a men's movement, which started in Holland in 2008, and now has branches in twelve countries. It takes its name from D'Artagnan, the ambitious young soldier, in the novel by Alexandre Dumas, who aspires to join the elite troops of the king and become the 4th Musketeer.

In this book, Henk and Theo describe how you too can become a hero in the service of the King. They outline the various challenges that face men today; who's in charge? How do you find your potential? What is worth living for? What does God have to do with it? Specific chapters address themes such as money, power, lust and forgiveness.

4M offers popular and extreme character-building experiences based around a 72-hour mind, body and soul adventure and even tougher 'Muskathlons'. These remind men of their great potential, connect them closer to each other and their God and offer them the chance to fight against injustice on a global stage.

Henk Stoorvogel is a pastor in the Netherlands, and founder of Athletes in Action. Theo van den Heuvel was for five years director of Athletes in Action, and is also a pastor. Both have an extensive speaking ministry.

To find 4M in your country:

4M USA (also covers Guatemala):   www.the4thmusketeer.org
4M United Kingdom: www.the4thmusketeer.uk
4M South Africa: www.the4thmusketeer.co.za
4M The Netherlands: www.de4emusketier.nl
4M Belgium: www.de4emusketier.be
4M Suisse: www.der4temusketier.ch
4M Germany: www.der4temusketier.de
4M Norway: www.the4thmusketeer.no
4M Poland: www.4muszkieter.pl
4M Australia: www.the4thmusketeer.com.au
4M Austria: www.der4temusketier.at

And to check out your Muskathlon, visit www.muskathlon.com